Kaleidoscope

Level E

Decodable Stories and Spelling

SRA

Columbus, OH

The McGraw·Hill Companies

SRAonline.com

 SRA

Send all inquiries to this address:
SRA/McGraw-Hill
4400 Easton Commons
Columbus, OH 43219

ISBN: 978-0-07-614346-7
MHID: 0-07-614346-5

1 2 3 4 5 6 7 8 9 QPD 13 12 11 10 09 08 07

Table of Contents

Unit 1

Unit 2

Table of Contents

Unit
3

Table of Contents

Unit 4

Unit 5

Table of Contents

Unit 6

Decodable Stories and Spelling

Name _____ Date _____

Unit 1 • *Save the Glen!*

1. _____ jam

2. _____ hat

3. _____ dash

4. _____ path

5. _____ fed

6. _____ bells

7. _____ test

8. _____ send

9. _____ hit

10. _____ fix

11. _____ winner

12. _____ trip

13. _____ cot

14. _____ mop

15. _____ shop

16. _____ spot

17. _____ muddy

18. _____ bug

19. _____ truck

20. _____ shut

Name _____ Date _____

Unit 1 • *Save the Glen!*

**Proofread each sentence below. Each has a Spelling
word in it. Circle the Spelling word, and then write
its correct spelling on the line.**

1. I shutt the window when it started to rain. _____

2. The man unloaded boxes from the truck. _____

3. A bugg is crawling on the floor. _____

4 Collin has muddy shoes. _____

5. There is a sput on my new shirt. _____

6. This shop has nice clothes. _____

7. After lunch, I will mip the floor. _____

8. Jack can sleep on the cott. _____

9. I would like to take a trop to Florida. _____

10. Our team hopes to be the winerr of the tournament. _____

11. The mechanic will fex our car quickly. _____

12. It isn't nice to hot other people. _____

13. We will send Ally some flowers for her birthday. _____

14. I thought the tast was difficult. _____

15. The bels are ringing. _____

16. The baby has been fid. _____

17. Follow the poth so you don't get lost. _____

18. The stew needs a desh of pepper and salt. _____

19. Your hut is on the table. _____

20. Sandy made strawberry jamm. _____

Name _____ Date _____

Unit 1 • *Save the Glen!* • STORY 1

I am Snap. I am an ant.	1–7
Pat is a man. Pat sat at the tan mat. A ham is at the	8–22
tan mat.	23–24
I sat at the tan mat. I tap Pat.	25–33
"Pass the ham, Pat."	34–37
I am Sam. I am a man.	38–44
Snap is an ant. Snap is at the tan mat. A ham is at the	45–59
tan mat.	60–61
I sat at the mat. I tap Snap.	62–69
"Pass the ham, Snap."	70–73
I am Pam. I am an ant.	74–80
Sam is a man. Sam is at the tan mat. A ham is at the	81–95
tan mat.	96–97
I sat at the mat. I tap Sam.	98–105
"Pass the ham, Sam."	106–109
I am Pat. I am a man.	110–116
Pam is an ant. Pam is at the tan mat. A ham is at the	117–131
tan mat.	132–133
I sat at the mat. I tap Pam.	134–141
"Pass the ham, Pam."	142–145
Pass the ham to Snap, Sam, Pam, and Pat.	146–154

I read this
○ silently.   ○ aloud.   ○ with a partner.   ○ with the teacher.

Unit 1 • *Save the Glen!* • Story 2

Deb and Dad sell hats at a stand.	1–8
Matt is at the stand. Deb and Dad hand hats to Matt.	9–20
Matt tests hats. Deb and Dad hand Matt ten hats. Matt	21–31
tests ten hats. Deb hands Matt a tan hat. The tan hat is	32–44
the last hat at the stand. Deb and Dad sell Matt the tan	45–57
hat.	58–58
Nell is a pet Lab. Nell is Matt's pet Lab. At a tent, Nell	59–72
naps. At a tent, Matt sets the tan hat at a mat.	73–84
Nell naps and naps. Pests land on Nell. Nell snaps at	85–95
the pests, steps at the mat, and stamps the hat. Splat! The	96–107
tan hat is a mess.	108–112
Matt is sad. Nell is sad. The tan hat is a mess.	113–124

I read this
○ silently.   ○ aloud.   ○ with a partner.   ○ with the teacher.

Unit 1 • *Save the Glen!*

Cut out the boxes on this page to make your own
set of Sight Word cards. The following Sight Words
are reviewed in this lesson.

a Unit 1, Lesson 1	**the** Unit 1, Lesson 1
and Unit 1, Lesson 1	**to** Unit 1, Lesson 1
I Unit 1, Lesson 1	Unit 1, Lesson 1
is Unit 1, Lesson 1	Unit 1, Lesson 1

Unit 1 • *The Odd Squad*

Cut out the boxes on this page to make your own
set of Sight Word cards. The following Sight Words
are reviewed in this lesson.

are Unit 1, Lesson 6	**she** Unit 1, Lesson 6
has Unit 1, Lesson 6	**you** Unit 1, Lesson 6
he Unit 1, Lesson 6	Unit 1, Lesson 6
on Unit 1, Lesson 6	Unit 1, Lesson 6

DECODABLE STORIES AND SPELLING

Unit 1 • *The Odd Squad*

1. _____ mask

2. _____ napping

3. _____ digging

4. _____ denial

5. _____ pencil

6. _____ lamb

7. _____ bath

8. _____ singing

9. _____ telling

10. _____ best

11. _____ local

12. _____ hands

13. _____ help

14. _____ limbs

15. _____ mend

16. _____ nest

17. _____ sand

18. _____ past

19. _____ terminal

20. _____ back

Unit 1 • *The Odd Squad*

Proofread each sentence below. Each has a Spelling word in it. Circle the Spelling word, and then write its correct spelling on the line.

1. My hannds are dirty. _____

2. Josh likes to halp his mother cook. _____

3. A person's arms and legs are called limbs. _____

4. He should mind the hole in your coat. _____

5. There are three baby birds in the nist. _____

6. The sand is very hot. _____

7. We walked passt Nick's house. _____

8. The bus terminel is very crowded. _____

9. I have to go bak to the dentist next week. _____

10. The masc has covered her eyes. _____

11. Mia is diging a hole for the flowers. _____

12. A pencil rolled onto the floor. _____

13. Kelly gave the dog a beth. _____

14. Michael likes teling you secrets. _____

15. We went to a local restaurant for dinner. _____

16. This is the bast apple pie I have ever tasted. _____

17. She likes singging in the choir. _____

18. My favorite nursery rhyme is "Mary Had a Little Lam." _____

19. My sister's dinial was very definite. _____

20. My father is naping on the couch. _____

DECODABLE STORIES AND SPELLING

Name _____ Date _____

Matt had on tan slacks and a black cap. He sat on a	1–13
pad on the back deck and had a picnic of snacks.	14–24
Nell, the pet Lab, slept on the sand. Nell can smell the	25–36
snacks. Nell sits. Nell has a plan.	37–43
Nell is on the steps. Nell is on the deck. Nell is on the	44–57
pad on the deck.	58–61
Can Matt pat Nell, the pet Lab? Matt sets the snack on	62–73
the pad. Matt pats Nell. Matt's hand is on Nell.	74–83
Nell can smell the snack on the deck. Nell has the	84–94
snack! Is Nell on the pad? Nell is past the pad. Is Nell on	95–108
the steps? Nell is past the steps! Is Nell on the sand? Nell	109–121
is on the sand. Nell has sped to the sand.	122–131
At last, Nell has a snack. Matt's snack is on the sand.	132–143
Matt is on the deck.	144–148

I read this
○ silently.   ○ aloud.   ○ with a partner.   ○ with the teacher.

Matt and Kim are on the deck. Kim has a can of skim	1–13
milk. Kim sips the skim milk. She sets it on the deck.	14–25
Nell, the pet Lab, sits on the deck. Nell tips the can	26–37
of skim milk. The can is on the deck. The milk is on the	38–51
deck and on the back steps. Specks of milk hit Matt's tan	52–63
slacks. Nell licks the spilled milk on the deck.	64–72
Matt and Kim tell Nell, "You scat, Nell!"	73–80
Nell scats and slips on the spilled milk on the slick	81–91
deck. She slips and hits a plant stand on the deck. Bam!	92–103
The plant stand hits the deck. Bits of the plant land on	104–115
Matt's tan slacks. Matt stands! "Scat, Nell!"	116–122
Nell slips on the spilled milk on the steps. Nell slips	123–133
on the slick steps. Splat! She hits the sand. The sand is	134–145
damp! She stands and scats. She kicks specks of sand	146–155
back on Matt. The specks of sand hit Matt's black cap	156–166
and tan slacks.	167–169
Matt is a mess. The deck is a mess.	170–178

I read this
○ silently.   ○ aloud.   ○ with a partner.   ○ with the teacher.

Name _____ Date _____

Unit 1 • *Gunther the Grouch*

1. _____ kick

2. _____ error

3. _____ stick

4. _____ importance

5. _____ cash

6. _____ barking

7. _____ photograph

8. _____ dark

9. _____ tracked

10. _____ photogenic

11. _____ creator

12. _____ disturbance

13. _____ hook

14. _____ inventor

15. _____ park

16. _____ assistance

17. _____ kept

18. _____ cracked

19. _____ allowance

20. _____ shock

Name _____ Date _____

Unit 1 • *Gunther the Grouch*

Proofread each sentence below. Each has a Spelling word in it. Circle the Spelling word, and then write its correct spelling on the line.

1. Our neighbor's dog is always barcking. _____

2. I will pay here in caash. _____

3. The importence of this invention cannot be overlooked. _____

4. Ben broke the stick in half. _____

5. There's an eror in this newspaper article. _____

6. Can you kik the ball to me? _____

7. Dragging your feet on the carpet will give you a shok. _____

8. I am saving my alowance to buy a bicycle. _____

9. My new vase is crakked. _____

10. Do you know where the cookies are kept? _____

11. If you get lost, ask a police officer for assistence. _____

12. We live next to a parck. _____

13. Who was the inventar of electricity? _____

14. Put your coat there on the hoock. _____

15. What is the cause of this disturbence? _____

16. I saw the cartoon's creator on television. _____

17. My mother is fotogenic and always looks good in pictures. _____

18. We cleaned up the snow as we trakked it into the house. _____

19. Susan needs to be home before darck. _____

20. Did you take a photograph of the wedding? _____

The tent sat on a cliff hidden in the damp mist. Greg	1–12
had slept a bit. When a wet drip hit the back of Greg's	13–25
neck, he sat up. He felt a rip in the tent. Greg lit the camp	26–40
lamp and filled the rip with a rag.	41–48
In the dim tent, Greg set back the wet tent flap. The	49–60
mist hid the cliff.	61–64
Greg had a big map. He held it to the lamp. He hit a	65–78
black speck on the map. "I am here."	79–86
Greg slid the map a bit. It had a red speck on it. He hit	87–101
it. "I want to get there. It is west."	102–110
When Greg sat on the mat in the tent, he had the last	111–123
snack left in his backpack. It was a scrap of ham and	124–135
milk.	136–136
Greg had to stick the tent and mat in the backpack.	137–147
The camp lamp went on a belt strap. He kept the map in	148–160
his hand.	161–162
Greg left in the wet mist. He left the cliff and went	163–174
west. "I will get there. I plan to get there."	175–184

I read this
○ silently.   ○ aloud.   ○ with a partner.   ○ with the teacher.

As Greg went west he spotted a hill. Greg went west	1–11
on the hill. He slid and fell a bit in the wet grass. He did	12–26
not stop. When he got past the hill, the mist had left. At	27–39
a big rock, he had a rest and held the map in his hand.	40–53
"This rock is on the map."	54–59
Past the big rock, Greg stepped in sand. In the sand	60–70
he spotted prints. Greg knelt at the prints. "What is this?	71–81
Did a fox step here? Did a dog step here?"	82–91
The prints led to a log. Next to this log sat a black and	92–105
tan dog. The dog ran to Greg. The dog let Greg pet it. The	106–119
dog had a tag. The dog is Max.	120–127
Max led Greg on a trek in the hot sand. In the sand,	128–140
Greg spotted a red knit hat. "Sam left this hat here," Greg	141–152
said.	153–153
Max ran and ran in the sand. Greg ran and ran. Greg	154–165
and Max had to rest. Greg held the map. "On the map is	166–178
the camp. Can I get to the camp?"	179–186

I read this
○ silently.   ○ aloud.   ○ with a partner.   ○ with the teacher.

Unit 1 • *Gunther the Grouch*

Cut out the boxes on this page to make your own set of Sight Word cards. The following Sight Words are reviewed in this lesson.

as Unit 1, Lesson 11	**this** Unit 1, Lesson 11
here Unit 1, Lesson 11	**what** Unit 1, Lesson 11
of Unit 1, Lesson 11	 Unit 1, Lesson 11
there Unit 1, Lesson 11	 Unit 1, Lesson 11

Name _____ Date _____

Unit 1 • *The American Dream: City or Suburb?*

Cut out the boxes on this page to make your own
set of Sight Word cards. The following Sight Words
are reviewed in this lesson.

her

Unit 1, Lesson 16

was

Unit 1, Lesson 16

his

Unit 1, Lesson 16

were

Unit 1, Lesson 16

said

Unit 1, Lesson 16

Unit 1, Lesson 16

see

Unit 1, Lesson 16

Unit 1, Lesson 16

DECODABLE STORIES AND SPELLING

Unit 1 • *The American Dream: City or Suburb?*

1. _____ waxed

2. _____ foggy

3. _____ nickel

4. _____ crooked

5. _____ buffet

6. _____ white

7. _____ liberated

8. _____ exit

9. _____ knocked

10. _____ rock

11. _____ stopped

12. _____ whispered

13. _____ front

14. _____ expert

15. _____ whined

16. _____ knotted

17. _____ expense

18. _____ rotten

19. _____ whale

20. _____ grow

Unit 1 • _The American Dream: City or Suburb?_

Proofread each sentence below. Each has a Spelling word in it. Circle the Spelling word, and then write its correct spelling on the line.

1. I found a big rok in the garden. _____

2. The strong winds nocked down the tree. _____

3. After the concert, the audience began to eksit the theater. _____

4. The prisoners were libarated from jail. _____

5. The fence needs to be painted white. _____

6. Jenny set up the bufet for her party. _____

7. The line I drew is croked. _____

8. Which president do you see on the nickel? _____

9. It is often fogy in London. _____

10. Steve said he just waksed his car. _____

11. My grandmother is going to gro tomatoes in her garden. _____

12. Someday I would like to go wale watching. _____

13. We have had roten weather this summer. _____

14. An exxpense is the amount of money spent on something. _____

15. This thread is knoted. _____

16. My little brother whined because he wanted candy. _____

17. I want to ask your exxpert opinion about something. _____

18. The frunt door is painted red. _____

19. Cody wispered something to his sister. _____

20. She stopped to get ice cream before going home. _____

Name _____ Date _____

The sun and sand were hot. Greg and Max had to get   1–12
a drink. "I cannot run in the sand and sun, Max," said   13–24
Greg. "I am such a wreck. I must rest."   25–33

Greg sat on a stump. Max sat next to him. Greg slid   34–45
on the sand and slept. This was bad! Max had to get Greg   46–58
to get up. Max had to tug at Greg's wrist. Max had to lick 59–72
Greg's chin.   73–74

Max did it! Max got Greg to get up. Greg held the map   75–87
up in the sun. "The camp is on a hill next to this sand.   88–101
Which hill? Can I spot it?"   102–107

He did. There were a bunch of tents and huts on top   108–119
of a hill. "Max, let's run up and see the camp!"   120–130

Greg and Max ran to the camp. "Greg, you are here!"   131–141
Sam said.   142–143

"That was my plan!" said Greg with a grin. He handed   144–154
Sam her red hat.   155–158

Sam had Greg sit at a bench in a tent. Max sat next to   159–172
him. Greg and Max had a big drink and a big snack. Then   173–185
Greg and Max had a bath and a nap. Greg slept and slept.   186–198
Max slept next to him.   199–203

Greg and Sam were pals.   204–208

I read this
○ silently.   ○ aloud.   ○ with a partner.   ○ with the teacher.

Phil was still in bed. The sun was not up. Dad crept up
to Phil and tapped his hand. "Let's catch a bunch of fish!"
he said.

Phil sat up. It was six o'clock. He did a stretch and
said, "Let's catch Big Ben Bass, Dad!" Big Ben Bass was
the biggest fish in the pond. It was bigger than a dolphin!

Dad and Phil went to the pond. It was spring, and
wrens sang. Dad and Phil had a long box. In the box were
fishing rods and a string net. Dad and Phil set up the rods
in the pond and shut the box.

Then Dad sat on a bench, and Phil sat on the sand.
Dad slept a bit, and Phil slept a lot.

Big Ben Bass swam in the pond. Big Ben Bass did not
let Dad and Phil catch him.

When Dad and Phil had lunch, there was a splash. Big
Ben Bass sprang up in the pond. "Dad, is Big Ben Bass
grinning at us?" asked Phil.

Then Big Ben knocked the rods in the pond. Dad had
to fetch the rods with the string net.

Dad and Phil were not a match for Big Ben.

1–13
14–25
26–27
28–39
40–50
51–62
63–73
74–86
87–99
100–106
107–118
119–127
128–139
140–145
146–156
157–168
169–173
174–184
185–192
193–202

I read this
○ silently.   ○ aloud.   ○ with a partner.   ○ with the teacher.

Unit 1 • *Pete Seeger: A Hero for All Seasons*

1. _____ skunk

2. _____ bookshelf

3. _____ search

4. _____ hung

5. _____ ballet

6. _____ policies

7. _____ peach

8. _____ clutched

9. _____ write

10. _____ string

11. _____ pretzel

12. _____ think

13. _____ watch

14. _____ eggshell

15. _____ graph

16. _____ sink

17. _____ political

18. _____ cheese

19. _____ fresh

20. _____ stitch

Unit 1 • *Pete Seeger: A Hero for All Seasons*

Proofread each sentence below. Each has a Spelling word in it. Circle the Spelling word, and then write its correct spelling on the line.

1. I can't get the knot out of your stringg. _____

2. Someday I would like to rite a novel. _____

3. The little girl cluched her mother's hand tightly. _____

4. She made the peatch cobbler I like. _____

5. The group's polisies are well known. _____

6. On Saturday we are going to the ballet. _____

7. I hungg a poster on my wall. _____

8. We went in seartch of our missing dog. _____

9. He found a book on the bookshelff to read. _____

10. That awful smell meant that a skunck was nearby. _____

11. Will you stitch the hole in my pants? _____

12. Let's take a walk and get some frech air. _____

13. I made a ham and cheese sandwich for you. _____

14. Our uncle is running for politicel office. _____

15. Do you wash your hands in the sinck? _____

16. This graff shows the company's profits. _____

17. Go crack the egshell with a knife. _____

18. A babysitter is going to wach us tonight. _____

19. Do you thinck they will come to my party? _____

20. They would like to have a pretzel. _____

Mom was in the car. She had lots to do. She had to get	1–14
a card and yarn at Jill's Shop. Mom did not see a spot to	15–28
park on the block at the card shop. She went to the next	29–41
block. There she started to park at Jeff's Garden Shop.	42–51
A man yelled at Mom. "You cannot park your car here. A	52–63
large truck must park here," he said.	64–70
Mom went to the next block and started to park at the	71–82
edge of Bridge Park. A man yelled at Mom, "You cannot	83–93
park here unless you are a judge at the Bridge Park Art	94–105
Contest." Mom was not a judge.	106–111
Mom went to the next block and started to park at the	112–123
farmers' market. A man yelled at Mom, "You cannot park	124–133
here. A big cart that is bringing stuff from a barn has to	134–146
park here."	147–148
Mom went to her yard and parked. "Jill's Shop is not	149–159
far," she said. "It is hard to park on the blocks at the	160–172
shop. I will just jog to the shop."	173–180
Mom dressed in her jogging top and pants and jogged	181–190
to Jill's shop. Mom is smart not to park at the shop.	191–202

I read this
○ silently.   ○ aloud.   ○ with a partner.   ○ with the teacher.

Dad, Mom, and Gina went to Gem Circus. Ginger was	1–10
sick and did not go. She had picked up a germ in class.	11–23
Lots of kids in Ginger's class were sick. When Mom, Dad,	24–34
and Gina left, Ginger sat in the den with Grandma.	35–44
Dad, Mom, and Gina had fun. They liked the Gem	45–54
Circus Jazz Band. They clapped when strong girls zipped	55–63
up to the top of the tent to twist and turn on swings. They	64–77
were stunned when a large elephant did a jig in the dirt.	78–89
They grinned when men dressed like big birds and gerbils	90–99
did a skit. The gerbils' hats were red fur or fuzz. Dad,	100–111
Mom, and Gina were not sure which. Ginger was glad she	112–122
did not see that!	123–126
Ginger was sad that she did not go. But Dad got	127–137
Ginger a red Gem Circus shirt. Mom got her a Gem	138–148
Circus gerbil jacket with a zipper. Gina got Ginger a	149–158
black pencil. Printed on the pencil was "Gem Circus."	159–167
Gina looked at the gifts. "Next trip to the circus, I will	168–179
be sick. Then I will get stuff like this," she kidded Ginger.	180–191

I read this
○ silently.　　○ aloud.　　○ with a partner.　　○ with the teacher.

Unit 1 • *Pete Seeger: A Hero for All Seasons*

Cut out the boxes on this page to make your own set of Sight Word cards. The following Sight Words are reviewed in this lesson.

he Unit 1, Lesson 21	**they** Unit 1, Lesson 21
do Unit 1, Lesson 21	**your** Unit 1, Lesson 21
go Unit 1, Lesson 21	Unit 1, Lesson 21
like Unit 1, Lesson 21	Unit 1, Lesson 21

Unit 1 • *The Woman Who Dared to Be First*

Cut out the boxes on this page to make your own
set of Sight Word cards. The following Sight Words
are reviewed in this lesson.

any Unit 1, Lesson 26	**never** Unit 1, Lesson 26
been Unit 1, Lesson 26	**with** Unit 1, Lesson 26
for Unit 1, Lesson 26	Unit 1, Lesson 26
from Unit 1, Lesson 26	Unit 1, Lesson 26

DECODABLE STORIES AND SPELLING

Unit 1 • *The Woman Who Dared to Be First*

1. _____ circle

2. _____ action

3. _____ giraffe

4. _____ judge

5. _____ cinders

6. _____ wooden

7. _____ jazz

8. _____ harden

9. _____ large

10. _____ yard

11. _____ first

12. _____ giant

13. _____ motion

14. _____ juicy

15. _____ turn

16. _____ herd

17. _____ yellow

18. _____ taken

19. _____ zebras

20. _____ shorten

Name _____ Date _____

Unit 1 • *The Woman Who Dared to Be First*

Proofread each sentence below. Each has a Spelling word in it. Circle the Spelling word, and then write its correct spelling on the line.

1. Did you shortin your hair? _____

2. Zeebras live in herds. _____

3. Have you takin out the garbage for Mom? _____

4. The traffic light just turned yelow. _____

5. A heard is a group of animals. _____

6. Make a left tern onto Pine Street from Vine Street. _____

7. This watermelon is very juicey. _____

8. The crossing guard made a quick moshon with her arms. _____

9. Troy built a jiant train track in the playroom. _____

10. Harry had been first in line. _____

11. We have a swingset in the yerd. _____

12. Julie has a larj bruise on her arm. _____

13. Did any of the glue on your paper hardin? _____

14. We went to a jaz concert last week. _____

15. I never like to sit on the wooden bench in the park. _____

16. The sinders are still glowing. _____

17. Grace is a good juge of character. _____

18. We saw a baby jiraffe at the zoo. _____

19. They decided to put their plans into action. _____

20. The teacher asked the students to sit in a curcle. _____

Unit 1 • *The Woman Who Dared to Be First* • Story 11

Norm Villa was just a kid. He liked to perform on the	1–12
horn. In fact, when the Gem Circus Jazz Band's horn man	13–23
was sick, the band asked Norm to sit in. Norm was glad!	24–35
Norm had breakfast, and then at ten o'clock that	36–44
morning Norm practiced with the band. That's when a	45–53
bad thing happened. A circus horse stepped on Norm's	54–62
horn.	63–63
At seven o'clock, Norm sat on his porch. He had a red	64–75
Jazz Band cap on his head. He had on a red Jazz Band	76–88
vest and pants. But Norm was sad. He had the bent horn	89–100
on his lap.	101–103
"I wish we had a better horn for you, Norm," Mom	104–114
said.	115–115
Just then, a van zipped up and parked by the porch. It	116–127
was Gramps. He had with him a silver horn. It had been	128–139
Gramps's horn. It was the best horn in Fort Dodge. That's	140–150
where the Villas lived.	151–154
"Norm, I read the short message from your Mom on	155–164
the Internet," Gramps said. "I am sad that your horn is	165–175
bent. You can perform with this." He handed the silver	176–185
horn to Norm.	186–188
"I never expected this, Gramps!" Norm jumped up and	189–197
hugged Gramps.	198–199

I read this
◯ silently.   ◯ aloud.   ◯ with a partner.   ◯ with the teacher.

"A box of cheddar crackers is missing," said Mom.   1–9

"Any hints?" asked Dad.   10–13

"On the rug, there is a path of cheddar cracker   14–23
crumbs," said Mom.   24–26

Mom and Dad tracked the path past the steps into the   27–37
yard. The crumbs led to a big quilt on the bench next to   38–50
the swings.   51–52

"Is that a kid under the quilt?" asked Mom.   53–61

"Yes, and I think a dog," said Dad grinning.   62–70

With a quick snap, Dad whipped the quilt back. Tom   71–80
and Suds, the dog, were under it. Crumbs were on Tom's   81–91
chin and hands. There were crumbs on Suds's fur and   92–101
collar. There were crumbs on the quilt.   102–108

"Suds and I just had a snack!" said Tom.   109–117

"Yes, we can tell. There is a path of crumbs," said   118–128
Mom. "And if you spot a mirror, you will see crumbs on   129–140
your chin.   141–142

"Suds and I will work to fix the mess," said Tom.   143–153

Suds jumped up and licked up the crumbs in the yard.   154–164

"But I cannot do that!" said Tom.   165–171

"Just pets can, not kids," said Mom.   172–178

"Yes. Plus, I am sick of cheddar crackers!" said Tom.   179–188

Mom and Dad grinned.   189–192

I read this
○ silently.   ○ aloud.   ○ with a partner.   ○ with the teacher.

Unit 2 • *Digging Up the Past*

1. _____ dollar

2. _____ queen

3. _____ bread

4. _____ vacationing

5. _____ sport

6. _____ vine

7. _____ donor

8. _____ strengthen

9. _____ feathers

10. _____ work

11. _____ quicksand

12. _____ actor

13. _____ sailor

14. _____ invention

15. _____ valley

16. _____ threatened

17. _____ formal

18. _____ quality

19. _____ read

20. _____ color

Unit 2 • *Digging Up the Past*

Proofread each sentence below. Each has a Spelling word in it. Circle the Spelling word, and then write its correct spelling on the line.

1. Do you werk for the phone company? _____

2. Some of the bird's fethers are on the bottom of the cage. _____

3. I practice playing soccer so that I can strenthen my skills. _____

4. The donor gave money to build the park. _____

5. The arbor supports the vin. _____

6. Basketball is my favorite spert. _____

7. Our family enjoys vacashuning in Maine. _____

8. My aunt's homemade breed is delicious. _____

9. The Queen of England lives in Buckingham Palace. _____

10. This candy does cost a doller. _____

11. What coler are your eyes? _____

12. I red a magazine while I waited. _____

13. She is not happy with the qality of her new shoes. _____

14. We needed to wear formel clothes to the party. _____

15. How many animals are thretened to become extinct? _____

16. A small stream runs through the valley. _____

17. I have a great idea for an invenshun. _____

18. Megan is a good saylor. _____

19. Mason wants to be an aktor. _____

20. Be careful when you look at the quicksand. _____

Name _____ Date _____

Abe went to a yard sale. Mom gave Abe a bit of cash	1–13
to spend at the sale. Abe had a look at the things in the	14–27
yard. There was a stuffed ape that Abe liked. Next to that	28–39
was a vase. The tags on the ape and the vase said "ten	40–52
cents." Abe kept looking. He spotted some paper that can	53–62
be made into planes. The tag said "six cents."	63–71
"I'll take that paper that makes planes," Abe said to	72–81
the man running the sale. "Does it cost much?"	82–90
"That will be six cents," said the man.	91–98
Abe got the cash from his pocket. He ran back to his	99–110
place to make many paper planes. Abe had markers to	111–120
make the planes look sharp. He named the first plane	121–130
Agent Vapor. Then Abe made the next plane. He named	131–140
that plane *Space Wave.* Abe had fun making the paper	141–150
planes.	151–151

I read this
○ silently.   ○ aloud.   ○ with a partner.   ○ with the teacher.

Gail paid a visit to the main branch of the May Day	1–12
Clay Maker's Shop. Gail is an artist. Gail makes art with	13–23
clay. She went to the main branch to get eight big blocks	24–35
of clay. The shop will ship the clay to Gail's place by	36–47
freight truck.	48–49
The freight truck came on Sunday. Sunday was Gail's	50–58
best day for making art with clay. On this day, Gail made	59–70
a sleigh. She laid the sleigh on her art bench. Gail made a	71–83
train with clay as well. Then she made a plain tray, a cat	84–96
with a tail, and a big snail.	97–103
Gail had a bit of clay left. Here is how she finished it.	104–116
She made eight paperweights. The paperweights made	117–123
perfect gifts. She gave a paperweight to her neighbors.	124–132
Gail liked her art. The neighbors liked Gail's art.	133–141

I read this
◯ silently.   ◯ aloud.   ◯ with a partner.   ◯ with the teacher.

DECODABLE STORIES AND SPELLING

Unit 2 • *Digging Up the Past*

Cut out the boxes on this page to make your own set of Sight Word cards. The following Sight Words are reviewed in this lesson.

# does Unit 2, Lesson 1	Unit 2, Lesson 1
# look Unit 2, Lesson 1	Unit 2, Lesson 1
# how Unit 2, Lesson 1	Unit 2, Lesson 1
# many Unit 2, Lesson 1	Unit 2, Lesson 1

Unit 2 • *Early African Traders*

Cut out the boxes on this page to make your own
set of Sight Word cards. The following Sight Words
are reviewed in this lesson.

often Unit 2, Lesson 6	Unit 2, Lesson 6
once Unit 2, Lesson 6	Unit 2, Lesson 6
some Unit 2, Lesson 6	Unit 2, Lesson 6
want Unit 2, Lesson 6	Unit 2, Lesson 6

Name _____ Date _____

Unit 2 • *Early African Traders*

1. _____ bacon

2. _____ triangle

3. _____ stay

4. _____ quadruplets

5. _____ space

6. _____ unicycle

7. _____ ceiling

8. _____ way

9. _____ multivitamin

10. _____ snakes

11. _____ combination

12. _____ trail

13. _____ safe

14. _____ concert

15. _____ able

16. _____ eight

17. _____ complaints

18. _____ wait

19. _____ collect

20. _____ shade

Name _____ Date _____

Unit 2 • *Early African Traders*

Proofread each sentence below. Each has a Spelling word in it. Circle the Spelling word, and then write its correct spelling on the line.

1. This shaade of pink is my favorite. _____

2. Did the workers callect the garbage yet? _____

3. I had to wait ten minutes once before seeing the doctor. _____

4. Do you have any complants? _____

5. I went to bed at eit o'clock. _____

6. I was not abel to get in touch with him. _____

7. The musician gave a concert in the park often. _____

8. Is it saife to go outside? _____

9. There's a hiking trayl in town. _____

10. This color conbination looks nice. _____

11. We saw some snaakes at the zoo. _____

12. Taking a multyvitamin every day helps me stay healthy. _____

13. I think I'll do it my wa. _____

14. The ceiling needs to be painted. _____

15. A unisycle is a vehicle with one wheel. _____

16. Someday I want to travel to spaace. _____

17. My aunt just had quadruplets. _____

18. I think that I will sta home today. _____

19. The top of the building is shaped like a triangel. _____

20. I can hear the bacin sizzling. _____

Name _____ Date _____

Miss Pete asked the kids in her class to keep records.	1–11
The theme of Miss Pete's class this week was sleep. She	12–22
wanted to let the kids see how to get the best week of	23–35
sleep.	36–36
Steve kept track of when he went to bed in the	37–47
evening. He even kept track of what he had for dinner.	48–58
It seemed to Steve that when he ate a fat-free dinner, he	59–70
slept better. Maybe dinners with a lot of fat made him	71–81
feel restless. Steve liked a deep sleep.	82–88
Miss Pete graded Steve's sleep record. It was not a	89–98
secret that Steve did his best. He had three pages in his	99–110
sleep project. He even made some charts that he placed	111–120
between the pages. Miss Pete was impressed.	121–127

I read this
◯ silently.   ◯ aloud.   ◯ with a partner.   ◯ with the teacher.

Name _____ Date _____

Miss Pete's theme for the next week's class was	1–9
dreams. She had the class study the dreams they had.	10–19
Miss Pete said she believed that dreaming was neat.	20–28
Some dreams are easy to remember, and some are foggy.	29–38
She said not to treat bad dreams as real.	39–47
Miss Pete then asked whether the kids wanted to tell	48–57
the class of a dream they had.	58–64
"I had a silly dream once," said Steve. "In the dream,	65–75
I was standing in a wheat field. There were peach trees	76–86
in the field as well. There was a stream in the field, but it	87–100
was filled with peanuts. The leaves on the trees were not	101–111
really leaves. They were pieces of meat. It was a funny	112–122
dream."	123–123
Miss Pete liked hearing Steve's dream. "Dreams often	124–131
can be silly," said Miss Pete. Other kids wanted to tell of	132–143
dreams they had. Each kid in the class got to speak of a	144–156
dream he or she had. It was a neat class.	157–166

I read this
○ silently.   ○ aloud.   ○ with a partner.   ○ with the teacher.

Name _____ Date _____

Unit 2 • *The First Olympic Games*

1. _____ happy

2. _____ sleepless

3. _____ evening

4. _____ inactive

5. _____ playful

6. _____ unseen

7. _____ carefully

8. _____ tree

9. _____ these

10. _____ helpless

11. _____ illogical

12. _____ dream

13. _____ carried

14. _____ signature

15. _____ scene

16. _____ leaves

17. _____ team

18. _____ worried

19. _____ sneak

20. _____ feed

Unit 2 • *The First Olympic Games*

Proofread each sentence below. Each has a Spelling word in it. Circle the Spelling word, and then write its correct spelling on the line.

1. Their answer comments are ilogical. _____

2. I had a dream about you last night. _____

3. Julia carreed the grocery bags into the house. _____

4. This document requires your signiture. _____

5. We practiced this seen of the play yesterday. _____

6. You are not as helples as a baby. _____

7. Theese pants are too big. _____

8. The tre is losing its leaves every year. _____

9. Read the directions carefuly before you start the test. _____

10. Who is our new teacher who remains unseen? _____

11. I collected leeves for my collage. _____

12. Our team has lost two games this season. _____

13. My mother was worryd about me. _____

14. She tried to sneek a look at her present. _____

15. I like to fead the ducks at the park. _____

16. Nina is playfull and likes to have fun. _____

17. Nocturnal animals are enactive during the day. _____

18. This evning I am going to a party. _____

19. I had a slepless night because the dog's barking kept me awake. _____

20. Samantha was very happy to see us again. _____

Dad asked Mike whether he wanted to go for a drive.	1–11
They were going to pick up some pies. It was Mike's	12–22
birthday, and they were having a party. Mike was nine.	23–32
While Dad was driving, Mike smiled. He liked the winding	33–42
trails on which Dad had to drive.	43–49
It was a five-mile ride to the pie shop. On the way to	50–62
the pie shop, Dad and Mike passed an ice-cream stand,	63–72
a tire repair shop, and a shiny fire truck. The pie shop	73–84
was next to the place where Dad got Mike a tie for his	85–97
birthday.	98–98
At the pie shop, Mike and Dad looked at each of the	99–110
pies. "What kind of pie do you want this year?" asked	111–121
Dad. Mike checked all the pies lined up in the pie case. "I	122–134
have decided on the lime pie," answered Mike.	135–142
Dad got three lime pies. "Twenty-five bucks for three	143–151
pies," said the man who ran the pie shop.	152–160
When Mike and Dad got back, Mike was thrilled to	161–170
find his pals were waiting for him. It was a fine birthday	171–182
party.	183–183

> I read this
> ○ silently.　　○ aloud.　　○ with a partner.　　○ with the teacher.

Unit 2 • *The First Olympic Games* • Story 6

Mike got a lot of nice gifts for his birthday. He got a   1–13
kite that can fly high and then dive in the sky. He wanted   14–26
to try the kite at the party right on the spot. But Mom   27–39
said that might not be the best plan. She suggested he   40–50
wait until later.   51–53

Besides the kite, Mike got a flight jacket. It's the kind   54–64
of flight jacket that pilots have. Mike tried on the jacket.   65–75
It was just the right size. It was such a neat jacket that   76–88
Mike's pals had to try it on as well.   89–97

Finally, Mike got a flashlight for camping. Mike had   98–106
said that he liked to camp, but he did not have a nice   107–119
flashlight. When it is night in the forest, you really need a   120–131
light to see. This bright flashlight was perfect.   132–139

By the time the gifts were unwrapped, the pies were   140–149
sliced and ready to eat. The kids ate the pies, and then   150–161
went to play with Mike's kite. Mike had on his flight   162–172
jacket. The kite sailed high into the sky. When Mike   173–182
tugged the string, the kite dived. Then the kite sailed high   183–193
into the sky again. The kids yelled in delight.   194–202

Mike's birthday party had ended just right.   203–209

I read this
○ silently.   ○ aloud.   ○ with a partner.   ○ with the teacher.

Unit 2 • *The First Olympic Games*

Cut out the boxes on this page to make your own
set of Sight Word cards. The following Sight Words
are reviewed in this lesson.

again

Unit 2, Lesson 11

Unit 2, Lesson 11

answer

Unit 2, Lesson 11

Unit 2, Lesson 11

who

Unit 2, Lesson 11

Unit 2, Lesson 11

year

Unit 2, Lesson 11

Unit 2, Lesson 11

Unit 2 • *Legendary Stars*

Cut out the boxes on this page to make your own
set of Sight Word cards. The following Sight Words
are reviewed in this lesson.

enough

Unit 2, Lesson 16

Unit 2, Lesson 16

give

Unit 2, Lesson 16

Unit 2, Lesson 16

these

Unit 2, Lesson 16

Unit 2, Lesson 16

where

Unit 2, Lesson 16

Unit 2, Lesson 16

Unit 2 • *Legendary Stars*

1. _____ find

2. _____ poetic

3. _____ cry

4. _____ pilot

5. _____ untie

6. _____ right

7. _____ public

8. _____ night

9. _____ hide

10. _____ pie

11. _____ classic

12. _____ empower

13. _____ enable

14. _____ impress

15. _____ fly

16. _____ light

17. _____ instead

18. _____ subscribe

19. _____ fried

20. _____ like

Unit 2 • *Legendary Stars*

Proofread each sentence below. Each has a Spelling word in it. Circle the Spelling word, and then write its correct spelling on the line.

1. Would you like another slice of py? _____

2. You cannot hiede from me. _____

3. Are you free to give me a ride home tomorrow night? _____

4. My brother wants to wear these pajamas in publik. _____

5. I write with my rite hand. _____

6. Would you unty my apron? _____

7. The pielot landed the plane safely. _____

8. I tried not to crie after I fell. _____

9. Poitic language has qualities associated with poetry. _____

10. Lisa couldn't find where her homework was. _____

11. Dan does not lieke tuna fish. _____

12. Have you ever tried fryd green tomatoes? _____

13. Our family is going to subscrieb to the zoo. _____

14. Holly decided to wear her blue dress instead of the black one. _____

15. The lite is very bright. _____

16. Should we flie or drive to California? _____

17. The movie did not empress us enough. _____

18. The donated money will inable the community center to build a pool. _____

19. His mother tried to empower her son to do his best. _____

20. We are designing our home in the classik style. _____

Hope rode Smokey, her pony, to the edge of the	1–10
forest. Did Hope see a doe and baby doe in the trees? Yes,	11–23
it was a baby doe and a big doe. Hope tied Smokey to a	24–37
branch and crept closer. Hope hid behind a big stone and	38–48
studied the baby. The tiny thing shivered. Was it cold?	49–58
Hope felt sad for the tiny thing.	59–65
Hope spoke quietly to the baby doe. "Hello," she said.	66–75
"Are you cold? Your nose looks so cold."	76–83
The big doe turned to where Hope was and then	84–93
nodded at the baby. Both mom and baby broke into a	94–104
run, bolting over broken trees.	105–109
For some strange reason, Hope felt sad. "A baby doe	110–119
is supposed to be in the cold," she said to herself. "A doe	120–132
spends the year in the forest. I don't need to feel sad for	133–145
it."	146–146
Hope decided it was time to go home. She was getting	147–157
cold. Hope's toes were the coldest. They felt frozen! She	158–167
jumped on Smokey. They trotted home.	168–173
Hope told Mom the story of the does she spotted.	174–183
Mom told Hope that it was okay for these does to be in	184–196
the cold. And the baby was not by itself. The big doe was	197–209
close by. Still, when Hope was snug in her bed at night,	210–221
she dreamed about the baby doe shivering in the cold.	222–231

I read this
○ silently.   ○ aloud.   ○ with a partner.   ○ with the teacher.

Hope woke in the morning as the sun shone in her	1–11
window. She looked at the meadow between her home	12–20
and the forest. Last night, the meadow had been coated	21–30
with a bit of snow. Today the snow was not there. The	31–42
heat of the sun made the snow melt.	43–50
Mom yelled to Hope, "Breakfast is ready!" Hope made	51–59
her bed. She just had to throw her pillow on the bed and	60–72
she was set to eat.	73–77
Breakfast looked yummy. Mom made enough toast	78–84
and oatmeal for an army. Hope loaded her toast with	85–94
butter and jam. She ate fast.	95–100
"Eat slowly, Hope," said Mom.	101–105
"I need to give my pony her breakfast," said Hope.	106–115
After breakfast, Hope tossed on her coat, fed her	116–124
pony, Smokey, and then went for a stroll on the road.	125–135
There she spotted the does from the forest. The baby	136–145
was close, looking at a black crow that had flown onto a	146–157
perch on the fence. Hope was happy to see the does. This	158–169
was a nice start to the day.	170–176

I read this
○ silently.   ○ aloud.   ○ with a partner.   ○ with the teacher.

Unit 2 • *Ancients in the Andes*

1. _____ over
2. _____ toe
3. _____ clarity
4. _____ boat
5. _____ throw
6. _____ nervous
7. _____ note
8. _____ blow
9. _____ uniform
10. _____ monologue
11. _____ smoke
12. _____ doe
13. _____ multiplied
14. _____ snow
15. _____ electricity
16. _____ poisonous
17. _____ coat
18. _____ famous
19. _____ hold
20. _____ role

Unit 2 • *Ancients in the Andes*

Proofread each sentence below. Each has a Spelling word in it. Circle the Spelling word, and then write its correct spelling on the line.

1. He will play a major roole in planning the event. _____

2. The library will hoeld the book for three days. _____

3. A famous person is someone who is recognized by many people. _____

4. I left my cowt on the bus. _____

5. We saw a poisonus snake in the woods. _____

6. The power went out, and we don't have any electrisity in the house. _____

7. The snow made my hands very cold, so I will buy gloves. _____

8. It seems as if my chores have multiplyed since yesterday. _____

9. A dow is a female deer. _____

10. The smooke from the fire is bothering my eye. _____

11. Did you memorize your monalogue? _____

12. The nurse wears a white uniform. _____

13. I'm going to blo the biggest bubble with my gum. _____

14. My mother wrote a great noote to my teacher. _____

15. I am nervus about the test I have tomorrow. _____

16. Do not throe your dirty clothes on the floor. _____

17. The waves rocked the boet. _____

18. Clarity is clearness of expression. _____

19. Which tow did you hurt? _____

20. I am going ovir to Michael's house. _____

Unit 2 • *Ancients in the Andes* • Story 9

After lunch, Hope told her mom that she had spotted	1–10
the same does again.	11–14
"The baby was so cute," said Hope. "That tiny doe	15–24
looks so puny next to the big doe."	25–32
"Some does can grow to be huge," said Mom. "Just the	33–43
antlers on a buck can be huge."	44–50
"Can I make that cute baby doe my pet?" asked Hope.	51–61
"I don't think so, Hope," Mom said. "That doe is cute,	62–72
but a wild baby doe won't make a good pet for humans."	73–84
"Can a mule be a pet for humans?" asked Hope.	85–94
"A mule?" Mom giggled. "Why do you ask if a mule	95–105
can be a pet?"	106–109
"I just read a great mule story," said Hope. "It seemed	110–120
like it might be a cute pet if I can't have the doe."	121–133
"Well, I don't think we can keep a mule and a pony	134–145
here, Hope," said Mom. "But we can go over to Mr. Uber's	146–157
pet shop in University City. We can buy a cute puppy for	158–169
a pet."	170–171
"Yippee!" yelled Hope. "I'll name my puppy Doe!"	172–179

I read this
◯ silently.   ◯ aloud.   ◯ with a partner.   ◯ with the teacher.

Unit 2 • *Ancients in the Andes* • **Story 10**

Hope and Mom were riding in the truck to Mr. Uber's	1–11
pet shop. The shop was a few miles away.	12–20
"We're low on fuel," Mom said to Hope. She eyed a fuel	21–32
stop up the road. "We're going to stop over there to get	33–44
some more."	45–46
"Does this truck need fuel often?" Hope asked.	47–54
"It depends," said Mom. "Sometimes I use the truck	55–63
a lot and sometimes just a few times a week. If I use it a	64–78
lot, then I need to buy fuel a few more times."	79–89
"Will the fuel you buy here last us the rest of the way	90–102
to the pet shop?" asked Hope.	103–108
"It will. It will even last a few more days," explained	109–119
Mom.	120–120
Mom paid for the fuel, and she and Hope hopped back	121–131
into the truck.	132–134
"Just a few more miles to go," said Mom. Hope smiled	135–145
at Mom, thinking of the new puppy she was going to	146–156
have.	157–157

I read this
○ silently.   ○ aloud.   ○ with a partner.   ○ with the teacher.

DECODABLE STORIES AND SPELLING

Unit 2 • *Ancients in the Andes*

Cut out the boxes on this page to make your own
set of Sight Word cards. The following Sight Words
are reviewed in this lesson.

buy Unit 2, Lesson 21	 Unit 2, Lesson 21
eye Unit 2, Lesson 21	 Unit 2, Lesson 21
have Unit 2, Lesson 21	 Unit 2, Lesson 21
great Unit 2, Lesson 21	 Unit 2, Lesson 21

Name _____ Date _____

Unit 2 • *Keeping Track of Time*

Cut out the boxes on this page to make your own
set of Sight Word cards. The following Sight Words
are reviewed in this lesson.

color

Unit 2, Lesson 26

Unit 2, Lesson 26

come

Unit 2, Lesson 26

Unit 2, Lesson 26

door

Unit 2, Lesson 26

Unit 2, Lesson 26

learn

Unit 2, Lesson 26

Unit 2, Lesson 26

DECODABLE STORIES AND SPELLING

Name _____ Date _____

Unit 2 • *Keeping Track of Time*

1. _____ formulated

2. _____ Utah

3. _____ few

4. _____ information

5. _____ fuel

6. _____ united

7. _____ architect

8. _____ use

9. _____ archrival

10. _____ unicorn

11. _____ cute

12. _____ value

13. _____ continue

14. _____ animal

15. _____ jewel

16. _____ educational

17. _____ ukulele

18. _____ cubes

19. _____ curfew

20. _____ rescue

Name _____ Date _____

Unit 2 • *Keeping Track of Time*

Proofread each sentence below. Each has a Spelling word in it. Circle the Spelling word, and then write its correct spelling on the line.

1. We helped rescew the boys from the river. _____

2. Do you have a curfue? _____

3. Would you like some ice cubes in your drink? _____

4. My grandmother plays the ewkulele. _____

5. This newspaper article is very educationul. _____

6. The color of the juwel sparkles in the sunlight. _____

7. A fox is a wild animal. _____

8. We will continu to play the game after dinner. _____

9. This watch has sentimental valew to me. _____

10. Your little brother is very cuete. _____

11. My favorite story has a unicorn in it. _____

12. In this story, the cat's arkrival is a dog. _____

13. Did you ewse the glue? _____

14. My father is an arcitect. _____

15. The workers were uwnited in their opinion. _____

16. Do we need ful for the car? _____

17. She went to the library to learn more infermation about dinosaurs.

_____

18. Only a fue inches of snow on the ground will come today. _____

19. I went skiing in Uetah. _____

20. We formulated our plans for the fundraiser and door prizes. _____

Mom and Hope drove over a hill and into a valley.	1–11
Above them on the next hill was University City. As they	12–22
drove into the city, all the homes looked alike to Hope.	23–33
She was used to the meadow and the forest. She had	34–44
never observed much of the city before.	45–51
"Is there a problem, Hope?" Mom asked. She noticed	52–60
Hope staring at the things in the city.	61–68
"No, Mom," said Hope. "I'm trying to learn about the	69–78
city. It's just so different here. Everything is going so fast.	79–89
What makes that happen?"	90–93
"Yes, things do seem fast in the city," Mom agreed.	94–103
"There is just so much going on across the city.	104–113
Everybody thinks they have to go quickly."	114–120
Hope nodded.	121–122
"It's just another few blocks to the pet shop," said	123–132
Mom.	133–133
Hope smiled again. They had come a long way to get	134–144
a puppy. Hope told Mom that she changed her mind. She	145–155
didn't want to name the puppy Doe. She was going to	156–166
name the puppy Alfalfa or Banana. She hadn't decided	167–175
yet.	176–176

I read this
○ silently.   ○ aloud.   ○ with a partner.   ○ with the teacher.

It was evening when Hope and Mom returned from | 1–9
the city. Hope had picked a puppy. She got a beagle. | 10–20
Hope decided to name the little beagle Rascal. Rascal | 21–29
was a total blast for Hope to play with. They ran across | 30–41
the meadow. Hope liked to tickle Rascal's tummy. Rascal | 42–50
wrinkled his nose when she did that. | 51–57

Once the baby doe was visible in the forest. Rascal | 58–67
stopped to look at it. Hope smiled as her puppy and the | 68–79
baby doe met each other. Hope felt that the doe needed a | 80–91
name as well. She felt that April was a good name for the | 92–104
doe. | 105–105

"April, I'd like you to meet Rascal," said Hope. "Rascal, | 106–115
I'd like you meet April." | 116–120

Rascal barked hello to April. April spotted a flower | 121–129
in the middle of the meadow. It was the color red. April | 130–141
went over to sniff its petals. Just then Mom yelled for | 142–152
Hope. | 153–153

"Hope, come on in," yelled Mom from the door. "We're | 154–163
having dumplings for dinner." | 164–167

Hope waved to April and picked up Rascal. She was | 168–177
going to have a lot of fun with her cuddly puppy. | 178–188

I read this
○ silently.   ○ aloud.   ○ with a partner.   ○ with the teacher.

Name _____ Date _____

Unit 3 • *Where the Chimps Are*

1. _____ coral

2. _____ travel

3. _____ sensible

4. _____ incapable

5. _____ dismissal

6. _____ twinkle

7. _____ council

8. _____ garden

9. _____ illegal

10. _____ bagel

11. _____ oral

12. _____ dental

13. _____ tunnels

14. _____ startled

15. _____ gentle

16. _____ banana

17. _____ multilevel

18. _____ illogical

19. _____ marvelous

20. _____ bottomless

Name _____ Date _____

Unit 3 • *Where the Chimps Are*

Proofread each sentence below. Each has a Spelling word in it. Circle the Spelling word, and then write its correct spelling on the line.

1. The judge could order a dismissil of the charges. _____

2. Young children are inncapable of taking care of themselves. _____

3. You should wear sensible shoes. _____

4. My grandparents like to travul around the country. _____

5. Corel is a marine animal that lives in colonies. _____

6. The boy should be gentul with his baby sister. _____

7. The loud noise would have starteld you. _____

8. There are two tunnals that lead into the city. _____

9. Please buy dental floss at the store. _____

10. The class listened to Brandon's orel report. _____

11. Laura is trying to dig a bottumless pit. _____

12. She looks marvalous in that dress. _____

13. His comments are illogical. _____

14. We live in a multilevul house. _____

15. Would you like a bananna? _____

16. She had a bagal and eggs for breakfast. _____

17. Illegul means against the law. _____

18. I planted carrots and zucchini in my garden. _____

19. Jason is running for student councel. _____

20. There's a twinkel in his eyes. _____

Name _____ Date _____

June asked Mom and Dad whether she could have a	1–10
sleepover for her pals. They said she could on Tuesday.	11–20
But there had to be some rules.	21–27
"The first rule," began Dad, "is that if anything gets	28–37
ruined, you have to pay for it."	38–44
"The second rule," said Mom, "is that you can't play	45–54
any cruel pranks. Some kids like to do that when they	55–65
have sleepovers."	66–67
"Okay," said June. "Nothing will be ruined. It's true	68–76
that some kids play cruel pranks, but we do not."	77–86
"The third rule," said Dad, "is to be nice to your sister,	87–98
Sue. You cannot be rude to her."	99–105
"I'm never rude to Sue," said June. "That's the truth."	106–115
"The last rule is the most important," said Dad. "Due	116–125
to the fact that Mom has so much tuna fish, you and your	126–138
pals should eat three tuna fish sandwiches each."	139–146
June looked at Dad. Then Dad started to giggle. Dad	147–156
was being silly with June.	157–161
"You don't have to eat tuna sandwiches," said Dad.	162–170
"The last rule is that you have fun."	171–178
June was truly relieved. She did not like tuna.	179–187

I read this
○ silently.　　○ aloud.　　○ with a partner.　　○ with the teacher.

June's pals would be arriving soon. June was getting   1–9
everything ready for the sleepover. She wanted this to be   10–19
the coolest sleepover her pals had ever been to. June was   20–30
new at this, but she knew she could make it a lot of fun   31–44
with Mom and Dad's help.   45–49

First Mom made certain that June had plenty of food.   50–59
Mom got some treats from Scoop's, the ice-cream shop on   60–69
the corner. Scoop's had a new flavor of ice cream called   70–80
Kangaroo Smooth. It was a mix of cherry and banana.   81–90

Next June set up the room. She had extra goose   91–100
feather pillows that she placed in the room for her pals to   101–112
sleep on. She knew her pals would like them. She had a   113–124
stuffed goose and a stuffed rooster that she got at the zoo   125–136
gift shop. She placed those on the bed.   137–144

After the room was in order, June asked Mom whether   145–154
they could use the pool that night. She liked to swim   155–165
under the moon.   166–168

"You can use the pool as long as Dad and I are there,"   169–181
said Mom. That was fine with June. Just then, her pals   182–192
started to arrive.   193–195

I read this
◯ silently.   ◯ aloud.   ◯ with a partner.   ◯ with the teacher.

Unit 3 • *Where the Chimps Are*

Cut out the boxes on this page to make your own
set of Sight Word cards. The following Sight Words
are reviewed in this lesson.

could Unit 3, Lesson 1	Unit 3, Lesson 1
should Unit 3, Lesson 1	Unit 3, Lesson 1
would Unit 3, Lesson 1	Unit 3, Lesson 1
Unit 3, Lesson 1	Unit 3, Lesson 1

Unit 3 • *Coyotes in the City*

Cut out the boxes on this page to make your own
set of Sight Word cards. The following Sight Words
are reviewed in this lesson.

earn

Unit 3, Lesson 6

Unit 3, Lesson 6

move

Unit 3, Lesson 6

Unit 3, Lesson 6

other

Unit 3, Lesson 6

Unit 3, Lesson 6

Unit 3, Lesson 6

Unit 3, Lesson 6

DECODABLE STORIES AND SPELLING

Name _____ Date _____

Unit 3 • *Coyotes in the City*

1. _____ cruelly

2. _____ tune

3. _____ studio

4. _____ bluebird

5. _____ boots

6. _____ glue

7. _____ cool

8. _____ rudely

9. _____ knew

10. _____ ruby

11. _____ mood

12. _____ moonlight

13. _____ blue

14. _____ food

15. _____ roommate

16. _____ too

17. _____ stew

18. _____ soon

19. _____ student

20. _____ rules

Unit 3 • *Coyotes in the City*

Proofread each sentence below. Each has a Spelling word in it. Circle the Spelling word, and then write its correct spelling on the line.

1. Do not break the rools. _____

2. One student knew the correct answer that will earn a good grade.

   _____

3. They will be arriving sewn. _____

4. Would you like some beef stue? _____

5. I would like some popcorn to. _____

6. Who is your roommate? _____

7. This restaurant has good fod. _____

8. Should I wear my blu shirt? _____

9. The monlight is shining in my window. _____

10. Our teacher is in a happy mood. _____

11. Her parents gave her a roby ring for her birthday. _____

12. Larry knoow how to fix my bicycle. _____

13. She answered her mother's question roodely. _____

14. I am going to take a col and refreshing swim in the pool. _____

15. Did you glew these papers together? _____

16. Did you move my bots? _____

17. Bluebirds are songbirds related to robins. _____

18. She is taking ballet lessons at the other dance stoodio. _____

19. He was humming a catchy toon. _____

20. It's not nice to treat others crewlly. _____

June's pals were having fun at her sleepover. Mom let | 1–10
them cook. They decided to bake cookies. They made the | 11–20
cookies in different shapes. Some cookies looked like a | 21–29
foot, others looked like woolly sheep. | 30–35

After they cleaned the kitchen, the girls sat in the | 36–45
yard overlooking the pool. They talked about good books | 46–54
they had read. | 55–57

Then June's pal Brook told the girls that her dad took | 58–68
a job in Hookville with a factory that makes wooden | 69–78
shelves. He could earn a better living there. So her family | 79–89
was going to move. The girls were all sad that Brook | 90–100
would be leaving the neighborhood. June shook her head. | 101–109
She was really the saddest that Brook was leaving. But | 110–119
she understood. | 120–121

Brook had a notebook for addresses and phone | 122–129
numbers. Each of the girls wrote in the book. | 130–138

After some more chatting, the girls went to sleep. The | 139–148
next day, they gave Brook hugs goodbye. It took a long | 149–159
time for everyone to leave because they each told June | 160–169
that they had a good time at her sleepover. Brook said | 170–180
that when she got settled in Hookville, she would have | 181–190
the girls over for a sleepover. | 191–196

I read this
O silently.   O aloud.   O with a partner.   O with the teacher.

Unit 3 • *Coyotes in the City* • Story 4

Every day at noon, Woody took a good look at his	1–11
lunch. Mom made him lunch to take in his lunchbox.	12–21
Today Woody had a good ham sandwich and an apple.	22–31
Mom always made the sandwich just the right size so	32–41
Woody had room for the cookies she gave him.	42–50
After lunch, Woody went to his woodworking class.	51–58
Woody was making a footstool for his dad. He still had to	59–70
sand it to make it smooth. Woody took his time making	71–81
the footstool. He wanted it to look good. It was going to	82–93
look nice in the living room at home.	94–101
When the bell rang to end woodworking class, Woody	102–110
went to his locker to get his books. His next class was	111–122
cooking. He never knew what kind of food they were	123–132
going to cook next. Today they got to choose what they	133–143
wanted to make. The class decided to cook pizza in the	144–154
wood-fired oven. It was fun to be able to cook different	155–165
things. The best part was that everything tasted so good.	166–175

I read this
○ silently.   ○ aloud.   ○ with a partner.   ○ with the teacher.

Name _____ Date _____

Unit 3 • *The Lady Who Started All This*

1. _____ roots

2. _____ cook

3. _____ truly

4. _____ submarine

5. _____ good

6. _____ duty

7. _____ gloomy

8. _____ flew

9. _____ transformed

10. _____ looked

11. _____ ruin

12. _____ tuna

13. _____ threw

14. _____ pool

15. _____ brook

16. _____ interstate

17. _____ connects

18. _____ transfer

19. _____ combine

20. _____ tube

Unit 3 • *The Lady Who Started All This*

Proofread each sentence below. Each has a Spelling word in it. Circle the Spelling word, and then write its correct spelling on the line.

1. They had a good time at the fair. _____

2. The subbmarine began to surface. _____

3. My father put heavy-dooty carpet in the basement. _____

4. Do you like to measure when you cok? _____

5. The rots of a plant keep it anchored in the ground. _____

6. It was trooly wonderful to see them again. _____

7. We luked at the movie three times. _____

8. After her makeover, she was completely transformed. _____

9. We flue to Chicago last weekend with people from work. _____

10. The team looked glomy after they lost the game. _____

11. We had a picnic by the bruk. _____

12. Let's take a swim in the pol. _____

13. An inturstate is a highway that travels between two or more states.

    _____

14. Nina made only toona salad for dinner. _____

15. After years of neglect, the house had gone to roin. _____

16. They threw a party for their grandmother's birthday. _____

17. We brought the inner toobe to the pool. _____

18. They tried to conbine the old with the new in their house. _____

19. Matt and his family might transffer to Atlanta. _____

20. The stone pathway connects the house to the garage. _____

Name _____ Date _____

Dom's class had a brown pet mouse. Dom's teacher	1–9
allowed Dom to keep the mouse at his house for a few	10–21
days. Mom said okay, but his brother Sid didn't know	22–31
about the mouse.	32–34
This morning Dom took a shower and got dressed.	35–43
As he was hanging up his towel, Dom heard a loud shout	44–55
from the kitchen. Dom ran there and found Sid standing	56–65
on the table.	66–68
"Sid, come down," said Dom.	69–73
"Dom, there is a brown mouse running around the	74–82
kitchen!" howled Sid with a frown. He stayed on the table	83–93
and cowered.	94–95
Dom picked up the brown mouse.	96–101
"Sid, this is only my class's pet mouse," said Dom. "His	102–112
name is Chowder."	113–115
Sid came down from the table. "He's not a wild	116–125
mouse?" he asked.	126–128
"Nope," said Dom. "He came from downtown at	129–136
Clout's Pet Shop. You can help measure his food."	137–145
"Wow, Dom," said Sid. "I think I'll like Chowder."	146–154

I read this
○ silently.   ○ aloud.   ○ with a partner.   ○ with the teacher.

Sam and Jack liked to go down to the big meadow | 1–11
by the water tower in town. They liked to throw around | 12–22
a yellow plastic disk called a Fling-O. The meadow | 23–31
gave them plenty of space. "Give me a high throw," Sam | 32–42
bellowed to Jack. "That will allow me to make a jumping | 43–53
catch." | 54–54

Jack gave Sam a high throw. Sam seemed to grow by | 55–65
a foot as he jumped and grabbed the Fling-O. | 66–74

"Wow," yelled Jack. He was blown away at Sam's grab. | 75–84

"Now throw it low," said Sam. Jack did. It was so low | 85–96
that Sam dove down. Just before the disk hit the grass of | 97–108
the meadow, Sam grabbed the low throw. | 109–115

"Wow," Jack howled again. "That's quite a show! I | 116–124
didn't know you had such Fling-O power." | 125–131

Sam stood and took a bow for an imaginary crowd of | 132–142
people. | 143–143

Later, after Sam and Jack had grown tired, Sam said, | 144–153
"Let's go down to the Crow's Crown for a soda." | 154–163

The Crow's Crown was an ice-cream shop in town. | 164–172
Sam and Jack will go back to the meadow tomorrow to | 173–183
throw the Fling-O some more. | 184–188

I read this
○ silently.   ○ aloud.   ○ with a partner.   ○ with the teacher.

Unit 3 • *The Lady Who Started All This*

Cut out the boxes on this page to make your own
set of Sight Word cards. The following Sight Words
are reviewed in this lesson.

measure	
Unit 3, Lesson 11	Unit 3, Lesson 11
only	
Unit 3, Lesson 11	Unit 3, Lesson 11
people	
Unit 3, Lesson 11	Unit 3, Lesson 11
Unit 3, Lesson 11	Unit 3, Lesson 11

Name _____ Date _____

Unit 1 • *Our Friend the Bat*

Cut out the boxes on this page to make your own
set of Sight Word cards. The following Sight Words
are reviewed in this lesson.

become Unit 3, Lesson 16	Unit 3, Lesson 16
off Unit 3, Lesson 16	Unit 3, Lesson 16
Unit 3, Lesson 16	Unit 3, Lesson 16
Unit 3, Lesson 16	Unit 3, Lesson 16

Name _____ Date _____

Unit 3 • *Our Friend the Bat*

1. _____ allow

2. _____ mouthful

3. _____ grow

4. _____ enjoyable

5. _____ brown

6. _____ mountain

7. _____ loud

8. _____ flowers

9. _____ format

10. _____ slowly

11. _____ clown

12. _____ sound

13. _____ growled

14. _____ comfortable

15. _____ south

16. _____ formation

17. _____ power

18. _____ dough

19. _____ ground

20. _____ likable

Name _____ Date _____

Unit 3 • *Our Friend the Bat*

Proofread each sentence below. Each has a Spelling word in it. Circle the Spelling word, and then write its correct spelling on the line.

1. He will become tired if he doesn't walk sloowly home. _____

2. They changed the foremat of the presentation. _____

3. He gave her beautiful flowers for her birthday. _____

4. The lowd noise startled me. _____

5. There is snow on top of the mowntain. _____

6. Sandy has broun hair. _____

7. The party was very enjoyible. _____

8. We grow vegetables in the garden. _____

9. The title of the book is a mowthful. _____

10. Ella's parents will not allough her to go to the dance. _____

11. Our teacher is very likible. _____

12. The boys are rolling around on the grownd. _____

13. The cookie dow is in the refrigerator. _____

14. During the storm, the powwer went out. _____

15. The scientists studied the rock formation. _____

16. The house faces sowth. _____

17. I am not comfortible in these wet clothes. _____

18. The bear grouwled loudly as he ran off to the woods. _____

19. Late at night, there wasn't a sound in the house. _____

20. To become a clouwn, he wore big red shoes. _____

Unit 3 • *Our Friend the Bat* • **Story 7**

Because Augie liked to write stories, he wanted to	1–9
become an author when he grew up. Augie's latest story	10–19
was about a hawk.	20–23
The hawk could launch off a cliff and soar around	24–33
the sky. The hawk was making a nest on the cliff, so he	34–46
would haul twigs and straw in his strong claws to the	47–57
site of his nest. In the story, the hawk spent a long day	58–70
making his nest. He was exhausted. The hawk yawned.	71–79
A big tiger saw the hawk making his nest. He went	80–90
over to the exhausted hawk. The tiger's paws were	91–99
soft and the hawk did not hear him coming. The hawk	100–110
was yawning, and the tiger snuck up on the hawk. This	111–121
caused the hawk to jump.	122–126
Just then the hawk broke into a drawn out fit of	127–137
giggling. The hawk and the tiger were pals. The hawk	138–147
found it funny that he was startled in the middle of his	148–159
yawn. The tiger helped the hawk finish hauling twigs and	160–169
straw. The tiger carried things with his jaw. The story	170–179
ended happily.	180–181
If you would like the author to autograph the story,	182–191
just ask Augie.	192–194

I read this
○ silently.   ○ aloud.   ○ with a partner.   ○ with the teacher.

Name _____ Date _____

Today was bring-your-daughter-to-work day. Last   1–5
year Mom took Augustine to her job at the bank. Today   6–16
Dad took her to his job at the ballpark. Dad is a   17–28
pro-baseball player.   29–30

Dad and his daughter walked up the small hallway to   31–40
the dugout. When they walked onto the field, Augustine   41–49
thought, "What a fun place to work."   50–56

The game wasn't going to start for a while. Augustine   57–66
and her dad saw workers spread chalk on the field. They   67–77
walked to the wall in the outfield. Augustine took her   78–87
mitt. Dad threw her some baseballs, and she caught them.   88–97

There were other baseball players with their   98–104
daughters on the field. Dad said he ought to introduce   105–114
them to his daughter. The players and their daughters   115–123
talked for a bit. Then it was game time. All the daughters 124–135
had seats behind the tall wall where they could watch the 136–146
game.   147–147

The daughters called to their dads during the game,   148–156
"Nice hit, Dad!" or "Great catch, Dad!" The girls talked   157–166
about how glad they were that their dads brought them   167–176
to the game.   177–179

I read this
○ silently.   ○ aloud.   ○ with a partner.   ○ with the teacher.

Name _____ Date _____

1. _____ scrawny

2. _____ awful

3. _____ fought

4. _____ laudable

5. _____ tall

6. _____ naughty

7. _____ autumn

8. _____ small

9. _____ comfortable

10. _____ bawled

11. _____ launched

12. _____ walk

13. _____ bough

14. _____ cautious

15. _____ fallen

16. _____ caught

17. _____ sauce

18. _____ chalk

19. _____ talk

20. _____ thought

Name _____ Date _____

Unit 3 • *The Solar House*

Proofread each sentence below. Each has a Spelling word in it. Circle the Spelling word, and then write its correct spelling on the line.

1. I think the book has fallen off the shelf. _____

2. My mother is very cawtious when driving in the snow. _____

3. The baugh of the tree broke during the storm. _____

4. I would like to take a wallk after dinner. _____

5. We lawnched the boat into the water. _____

6. Billy cought the football and scored a touchdown. _____

7. The woman asked for my tomato sawce recipe. _____

8. The chalk broke when it fell on the ground. _____

9. My parents taught me not to tallk to strangers. _____

10. I thaught they were going to the library. _____

11. My parents are tall. _____

12. The firefighter's bravery is lawdable. _____

13. During the game, Dan and Mark faught over the ball. _____

14. I heard that movie was awwful. _____

15. The scrauny lion looked for food. _____

16. The child bawled when she had to go to bed. _____

17. My new shoes are not comfortuble. _____

18. My pants are too smal. _____

19. In auutumn, we like to go apple picking. _____

20. The nawghty puppy chewed up the carpet. _____

Unit 3 • *The Solar House* • Story 9

King Troy decided he wanted to take a trip to his	1–11
boyhood home. King Troy lived in the royal palace. His	12–21
boyhood home was in a town called Roysville. King Troy	22–31
was ready for the long voyage. He had employed some	32–41
of his loyal subjects to serve as his convoy. The convoy	42–52
would ride with King Troy to make certain his voyage	53–62
was safe.	63–64
The people of Roysville heard of the king's voyage. As	65–74
the royal convoy arrived in Roysville, people went out to	75–84
greet King Troy. It was a joy-filled day for King Troy and	85–96
his loyal fans. His home stood just as he remembered it.	97–107
King Troy had worried that it would have been destroyed	108–117
after all this time.	118–121
The convoy stopped in front of the house so King	122–131
Troy could go inside. The house was kept as a royal	132–142
landmark. That meant that everything inside was just as	143–151
it was when he left it. King Troy found his old toys. King	152–164
Troy enjoyed his trip to Roysville. He played with his	165–174
toys the whole way back to the royal palace. Even a king	175–186
can enjoy his boyhood toys.	187–191

I read this
O silently.   O aloud.   O with a partner.   O with the teacher.

Kim was a woman with a long list of things to do. She	1–13
had her choice of where to begin. She looked at her list:	14–25

Things to do today:	26–29
1. Take laundry to coin-operated laundry.	30–35
2. Oil the squeaky hinge on the front gate.	36–44
3. Add soil to the flower box.	45–51
4. Get foil for storing food so the food won't spoil.	52–62
5. Go to voice lesson.	63–67
6. Embroider new dress for tonight's dinner party.	68–75
7. Broil sirloins for tonight's dinner party.	76–82

Kim decided to close her eyes and point to her list.	83–93
She pointed to number three on the list. She grabbed a	94–104
bag of soil. She dumped the soil into the flower box and	105–116
tried to avoid spilling any.	117–121
After toiling all afternoon, Kim had finished	122–128
everything on her list except for number seven. She	129–137
invited her pals to join her for a dinner of broiled sirloin.	138–149
At the end of the party, Kim rejoiced. Her party was	150–160
a hit. Not a single pal who joined her for dinner was	161–172
disappointed.	173–173

I read this
○ silently.   ○ aloud.   ○ with a partner.   ○ with the teacher.

Unit 3 • *The Solar House*

Cut out the boxes on this page to make your own
set of Sight Word cards. The following Sight Words
are reviewed in this lesson.

heard Unit 3, Lesson 21	Unit 3, Lesson 21
woman Unit 3, Lesson 21	Unit 3, Lesson 21
 Unit 3, Lesson 21	Unit 3, Lesson 21
 Unit 3, Lesson 21	Unit 3, Lesson 21

Unit 3 • *Oil-Eating Creatures*

Cut out the boxes on this page to make your own
set of Sight Word cards. The following Sight Words
are reviewed in this lesson.

father	
Unit 3, Lesson 26	Unit 3, Lesson 26
mother	
Unit 3, Lesson 26	Unit 3, Lesson 26
Unit 3, Lesson 26	Unit 3, Lesson 26
Unit 3, Lesson 26	Unit 3, Lesson 26

DECODABLE STORIES AND SPELLING

Name _____ Date _____

1. _____ boy

2. _____ boil

3. _____ fiesta

4. _____ join

5. _____ siesta

6. _____ disappointed

7. _____ annoyance

8. _____ toy

9. _____ attractive

10. _____ choices

11. _____ loyal

12. _____ avoid

13. _____ ointment

14. _____ oysters

15. _____ coin

16. _____ festive

17. _____ spoiled

18. _____ enjoy

19. _____ appointment

20. _____ noise

Unit 3 • *Oil-Eating Creatures*

Proofread each sentence below. Each has a Spelling word in it. Circle the Spelling word, and then write its correct spelling on the line.

1. What are my choyces? _____

2. This deal is very attracteve. _____

3. The toiy is on the shelf. _____

4. A broken-down car can be an annoiyance. _____

5. The class was disappoiinted when the field trip was cancelled.

_____

6. I think I will take a siesta. _____

7. Would you like to joiin me for dinner? _____

8. The feesta will begin in three hours. _____

9. It takes a few minutes for the water to boyl. _____

10. The boy went fishing at the lake with his father. _____

11. There is a lot of noyse in here. _____

12. I'm going to be late for my appoyntment. _____

13. Did you enjoiy the movie? _____

14. The refrigerator is broken, and the food is spoyled. _____

15. The party was very festive. _____

16. There is a cooin on the floor. _____

17. Oiysters are usually eaten raw. _____

18. The doctor gave my mother oyntment for her wound. _____

19. She couldn't avoyd hitting the other car. _____

20. If someone is loyal, they are faithful. _____

Name _____ Date _____

Each and every April, Mike's family went on a family	1–10
trip. Last April, they went to Yellowstone Park. They	11–19
hiked all around Yellowstone. The April before that,	20–27
they took a rafting trip on a wide river in the state of	28–40
Tennessee. The river was huge. This April, the family	41–49
decided to go to a beach in Florida.	50–57
Mike and his sister, Gail, helped pack the family's	58–66
green van. Dad arranged to have a neighbor take in the	67–77
mail while they were away. It was a long drive to the east	78–90
coast of Florida. Mom packed a load of snacks for the	91–101
drive. They had tiny cheese blocks, ripe peaches, yellow	102–110
bananas, and peanut butter sandwiches cut into pieces.	111–118
They finally arrived at the place they had rented on	119–128
the beach. The place used to be the home of an old pal of	129–142
Dad's. Mike and Gail ran straight for the shore. Gail saw a	143–154
rainbow in the sky. The kids sat on the beach and played	155–166
in the sand. They were going to have so much fun with	167–178
Mom and Dad while they were at the park all week.	179–189

I read this
○ silently.   ○ aloud.   ○ with a partner.   ○ with the teacher.

Name _____ Date _____

King Troy announced to his loyal subjects that he was   1–10
going to have a party for the whole town. He decided he   11–22
would allow everyone to have the day off from work and   23–33
join him in the town square at noon outside the tower of   34–45
the royal palace.   46–48

King Troy took off his crown and his royal   49–57
embroidered robe for the day. He wanted to mix with the   58–68
crowd. People from the town and nearby towns came   69–77
down to the royal party.   78–82

There was a clown with a pet mouse that did tricks.   83–93
It caught tiny paper balls with its paws. It rode around   94–104
in a little car the clown pulled behind him. Every time   105–115
the mouse did a trick, the crowd showed its enjoyment   116–125
by rejoicing with loud shouting. King Troy pointed at the   126–135
clown and appointed him the new royal jester.   136–143

After the clown had finished his act, King Troy   144–152
handed out flowers to all the boys and girls. The crowd   153–163
enjoyed King Troy's outdoor party so much that they   164–172
showered him with cheers and shouts. There was not a   173–182
single frown in the crowd.   183–187

So King Troy throws a royal party every year as a gift   188–199
to all the towns in his kingdom for being so loyal.   200–210

I read this
○ silently.   ○ aloud.   ○ with a partner.   ○ with the teacher.

Unit 4 • *The Birth of Basketball*

1. _____   subzero

2. _____

    _____   insurance

3. _____   lately

4. _____   try

5. _____   feet

6. _____   over

7. _____   mule

8. _____   owner

9. _____   sneaky

10. _____   creative

11. _____   find

12. _____   valuable

13. _____   convenient

14. _____   cane

15. _____   underway

16. _____   show

17. _____   dream

18. _____   communicate

19. _____   lazy

20. _____   usually

Unit 4 • *The Birth of Basketball*

Proofread each sentence below. Each has a Spelling word in it. Circle the Spelling word, and then write its correct spelling on the line.

1. She had a creetive approach to the problem. _____

2. The mail usally arrives in the afternoon. _____

3. Which day is more convenient for our meeting? _____

4. Drew is an insurance agent. _____

5. Did you fiend what you were looking for? _____

6. She said, "Don't be lazy." _____

7. In the winter, Antarctica has subbzero temperatures. _____

8. Would you like a candy can? _____

9. My brother is five feat tall. _____

10. My grandmother gave me this valueable ring. _____

11. Lateley, I have been very tired. _____

12. The construction is underwa. _____

13. Please trie to be on time. _____

14. Did you enjoy the show? _____

15. The play is almost over. _____

16. Would you comunicate this information to them? _____

17. The owener of the house is Nathan Wood. _____

18. I can't remember my dreem. _____

19. If someone is sneeky, they are tricky and devious. _____

20. A mule is a cross between a horse and a donkey. _____

In the old yellow house on the ranch owned by Patch	1–11
Stone resides a dog named Goldie. The kids in the small	12–22
town of Cherryville are afraid of Goldie. They've heard	23–31
that Goldie is as big as a stove and blows smoke out of	32–44
his nose. Some people even say that Goldie chewed his	45–54
way out of the chain that attached him to the porch.	55–65
Then came the day when eight kids were playing	66–74
catch near the yellow house on Patch Stone's ranch.	75–83
Mitch's throw sailed over Chuck's mitt and landed next	84–92
to where Goldie was dozing. Mitch made the throw, so he	93–103
had to go get the ball.	104–109
Mitch snuck over the fence and inched closer and	110–118
closer to the ball. It was almost in his reach when	119–129
suddenly Goldie woke up. Mitch froze. Goldie raised his	130–138
head and opened his big mouth, exposing rows of sharp	139–148
teeth. Was this the end for Mitch? No! Goldie gave Mitch	149–159
a kiss! He licked Mitch's cheek. Those old stories about	160–169
Goldie were a joke. Old Patch Stone even came out later	170–180
and said hello.	181–183

I read this
○ silently.   ○ aloud.   ○ with a partner.   ○ with the teacher.

Name _____ Date _____

Everybody in town had misjudged Goldie. They 1–7
thought he was a huge, evil dog with strange powers. 8–17
Now Mitch and Chuck know that Goldie is just a big, 18–28
gentle dog that wouldn't hurt a flower. 29–35

The boys went to visit Patch Stone in his house on 36–46
a Saturday morning. Patch was planting flowers in his 47–55
garden. 56–56

"How are you, boys?" asked Patch. 57–62

"We're just fine," replied Mitch. "We came to take 63–71
Goldie out for a walk around town." 72–78

"How nice," said Patch. "I think he's down on the flat 79–89
brown stones at the side of the house." 90–97

Mitch and Chuck went around the house to find 98–106
Goldie. They found him with his head down by the 107–116
ground. Goldie was taking a nap shaded from the hot 117–126
June sun. Just then Goldie woke up. He jumped to his feet 127–138
and ran to the boys. 139–143

"Down, boy!" Mitch shouted at Goldie, shortly before 144–151
getting licked. Goldie sat down on the grass. Mitch and 152–161
Chuck crouched down to pet Goldie. They decided not to 162–171
take Goldie for a walk right then. Goldie was right. It was 172–183
too hot out! Mitch and Chuck just rested in the shade too. 184–195

I read this
○ silently. ○ aloud. ○ with a partner. ○ with the teacher.

Unit 4 • *The Birth of Basketball*

Cut out the boxes on this page to make your own
set of Sight Word cards. The following Sight Words
are reviewed in this lesson.

a Unit 4, Lesson 1	**the** Unit 4, Lesson 1
and Unit 4, Lesson 1	**to** Unit 4, Lesson 1
I Unit 4, Lesson 1	Unit 4, Lesson 1
is Unit 4, Lesson 1	Unit 4, Lesson 1

Unit 4 • *Klondike Kate "Goes for the Gold"*

Cut out the boxes on this page to make your own
set of Sight Word cards. The following Sight Words
are reviewed in this lesson.

are Unit 4, Lesson 6	**she** Unit 4, Lesson 6
has Unit 4, Lesson 6	**you** Unit 4, Lesson 6
he Unit 4, Lesson 6	 Unit 4, Lesson 6
on Unit 4, Lesson 6	 Unit 4, Lesson 6

Name _____ Date _____

Unit 4 • *Klondike Kate "Goes for the Gold"*

1. _____ sleigh

2. _____ store

3. _____ policy

4. _____ catch

5. _____ plowing

6. _____ hurt

7. _____ safe

8. _____ burn

9. _____ fetch

10. _____ playroom

11. _____ stack

12. _____ fireplace

13. _____ corn

14. _____ day

15. _____ ovation

16. _____ rake

17. _____ shortly

18. _____ more

19. _____ city

20. _____ cloud

Name _____ Date _____

Unit 4 • *Klondike Kate "Goes for the Gold"*

Proofread each sentence below. Each has a Spelling word in it. Circle the Spelling word, and then write its correct spelling on the line.

1. They will come home shortly. _____

2. We're expecting mor snow tomorrow. _____

3. Hillary is an insurance agent in a big citi. _____

4. That clowd looks like an elephant. _____

5. Our cheeks were red after the slay ride. _____

6. Would you like to come to the stor with me? _____

7. There's a stack of books on the shelf. _____

8. Has he lit a fire in the fire place? _____

9. The farmer is plouing his field. _____

10. She didn't mean to hert your feelings. _____

11. My mother put her jewelry in the saife. _____

12. Don't bern your hand on the iron. _____

13. She will follow the new policy. _____

14. I hope you are not going to catch my cold. _____

15. He went to fech his sunglasses. _____

16. Would you clean the play room? _____

17. We had curn for dinner. _____

18. What daay is your doctor's appointment? _____

19. Will received a standing ovation for his performance. _____

20. The rake is in the garage. _____

DECODABLE STORIES AND SPELLING

Unit 4 • *Klondike Kate "Goes for the Gold"* • Story 3

As it got later in the day, the June sun began to go	1–13
down. Mitch and Chuck left the shade and played with	14–23
Goldie near the garden. They played fetch with Goldie.	24–32
The boys would toss a stick, and Goldie would see it sail	33–44
and chase after it.	45–48
"Are you going to take Goldie for a walk on the trail?"	49–60
asked Mitch.	61–62
"Yes," said Chuck. "He still has energy to burn. Let's	63–72
go!"	73–73
The trail made its way around a nearby lake. The	74–83
boys decided that Goldie would like the trail. They	84–92
checked with Patch Stone to make certain it was okay. It	93–103
was.	104–104
Goldie liked the trail right away. He hopped over logs	105–114
and ran into the lake. He ate blades of grass on the trail,	115–127
but he didn't like the flavor. The boys jogged to keep up	128–139
with Goldie. Goldie was taking the boys for a walk.	140–149
Goldie saw things he'd never seen before. He saw a	150–159
frog, a snail, a bird, and different kinds of bugs. Then	160–170
Goldie saw a little snake. Goldie wagged his tail and	171–180
seemed a little afraid. As the snake slithered away, the	181–190
boys led Goldie back to Patch's place. Goldie enjoyed his	191–200
day with Mitch and Chuck on the trail.	201–208

I read this
○ silently.   ○ aloud.   ○ with a partner.   ○ with the teacher.

After Goldie's walk at the lake, Lucy Stone could see	1–10
that Goldie needed a bath. Lucy was Patch Stone's sister.	11–20
Lucy got a small tub she kept in the basement and placed	21–32
it on the cement driveway.	33–37
Goldie did not like baths. Lucy grabbed Goldie's collar,	38–46
but Goldie got loose. Lucy tried to catch Goldie. Mitch and	47–57
Chuck tried too. Goldie was quick. Then Lucy went to the	58–68
kitchen to get a doggie treat. She placed the treat on the	69–80
cement near the tub. Soon after that, Goldie came over to	81–91
the tub.	92–93
Lucy grabbed Goldie's collar and held tight. She	94–101
got Goldie into the tub and sprayed him with a bit of	102–113
shampoo. After Goldie was covered with shampoo, Mitch	114–121
used the hose to rinse Goldie off. Goldie shook his body,	122–132
splashing Lucy. Lucy was all wet. Even her face was	133–142
soaked.	143–143
Lucy dried off a bit and then continued to use the	144–154
towel on Goldie. Then Lucy groomed her clean pet. Just	155–164
then Goldie got loose again, ran across the yard, and	165–174
jumped the fence. He ran into the muddy brook near	175–184
Lucy's ranch. Lucy looked at Goldie and shook her head.	185–194
Goldie would need another bath! Chuck handed Lucy the	195–203
shampoo.	204–204

I read this
○ silently.   ○ aloud.   ○ with a partner.   ○ with the teacher.

DECODABLE STORIES AND SPELLING

Name _____ Date _____

Unit 4 • *Henry Ford and the Automobile*

1. _____ throat

2. _____ playing

3. _____ remembered

4. _____ arm

5. _____ began

6. _____ toiled

7. _____

   _____ renew

8. _____ swirls

9. _____ creases

10. _____ throw

11. _____ start

12. _____ legally

13. _____ appreciation

14. _____ shadow

15. _____ history

16. _____ design

17. _____ point

18. _____ health

19. _____ restrictions

20. _____ really

Unit 4 • *Henry Ford and the Automobile*

Proofread each sentence below. Each has a Spelling word in it. Circle the Spelling word, and then write its correct spelling on the line.

1. I really enjoyed dinner. _____

2. She cleared her throat before she spoke. _____

3. Let's sit in the shadow of the tree. _____

4. My grandfather has some dietary restrictions. _____

5. The deesign of the building is unique. _____

6. Jim grabbed my arrm. _____

7. The doctor said that I'm in good health as of today. _____

8. My mother told us not to throew balls in there. _____

9. Here is the music you must practice plaeing piano. _____

10. Legully, they are not allowed to speak about the matter. _____

11. We begann painting the walls in the parlor red. _____

12. For many hours, they toiled cleaning the backyard. _____

13. He is majoring in historie, but I don't know what college he's attending.

_____

14. The poynt on my pencil is sharp. _____

15. The carpet has blue swerls. _____

16. This gift is a token of our appreciashun. _____

17. I remembered where I left my keys. _____

18. I'm going to reenew this book from the library. _____

19. He made creases in the paper. _____

20. The meeting will staart in ten minutes. _____

As Goldie lay down for a nap, Chuck, Mitch, and	1–10
Patch sat on the porch. It was quiet. Patch made a quart	11–22
of lemonade.	23–24

"How did you get the name Patch?" asked Mitch. — 25–33
Patch sat back and took a huge drink of lemonade. — 34–43

"This is why, boys," said Patch. "A long time ago I — 44–54
was working for a fuel company. My job was to measure — 55–65
different units of fuel to be loaded on trucks and shipped — 66–76
all around the United States. Well, at the fuel company, — 77–86
we had a softball team. I would always rip the pants — 87–97
on my uniform when I slid into bases. I would go home — 98–109
and stitch a patch over the hole in my uniform. But I — 110–121
wouldn't always have cloth the same color as my pants. — 122–131
So sometimes I'd use a blue patch, sometimes I'd use a — 132–142
red patch, or sometimes I'd even use yellow or green. So — 143–153
people at the fuel company quickly started calling me — 154–162
Patch." — 163–163

"That's a good story, Patch," said Chuck. "I would like — 164–173
a nickname like that." — 174–177

"You have to earn a nickname," said Patch. "Someday — 178–186
you'll have one. I'm going to go make another quart of — 187–197
lemonade." — 198–198

I read this
◯ silently.   ◯ aloud.   ◯ with a partner.   ◯ with the teacher.

Mitch and Chuck spent the day in town. Patch Stone	1–10
had looked at a calendar and told them that his dog,	11–21
Goldie, had a birthday next Tuesday. The boys wanted to	22–31
get a present for Goldie.	32–36
"What should we get?" asked Mitch. The boys were in	37–46
a music store. "Does Goldie like jazz?"	47–53
"I don't think Goldie likes jazz," said Chuck. "I think	54–63
maybe we should head to the pet store."	64–71
The boys went into Fern's Pet Zone. Fern was standing	72–81
behind the counter scratching her head.	82–87
"Hi there, boys," said Fern. "Is there anything I can	88–97
help you with?"	98–100
Chuck told her about Goldie's birthday coming up.	101–108
"Here are the collars," said Fern. "I'll bet Goldie would	109–118
like a new leather collar. Or maybe a feather collar	119–128
instead."	129–129
The boys were puzzled. A feather collar sounded zany.	130–138
"I think the leather collar will be nice," said Chuck.	139–148
Mitch agreed. "How much for the leather collar?"	149–156
"Just five dollars and fifty cents," said Fern. The boys	157–166
paid for the collar and thanked Fern for her help. Fern's	167–177
Pet Zone was the perfect spot to find a gift for Goldie.	178–189

I read this
○ silently.   ○ aloud.   ○ with a partner.   ○ with the teacher.

Unit 4 • *Henry Ford and the Automobile*

Cut out the boxes on this page to make your own
set of Sight Word cards. The following Sight Words
are reviewed in this lesson.

as Unit 4, Lesson 11	**this** Unit 4, Lesson 11
here Unit 4, Lesson 11	**what** Unit 4, Lesson 11
of Unit 4, Lesson 11	 Unit 4, Lesson 11
there Unit 4, Lesson 11	 Unit 4, Lesson 11

Unit 4 • *And Away We Go!*

Cut out the boxes on this page to make your own
set of Sight Word cards. The following Sight Words
are reviewed in this lesson.

he

Unit 4, Lesson 21

they

Unit 4, Lesson 21

do

Unit 4, Lesson 21

your

Unit 4, Lesson 21

go

Unit 4, Lesson 21

Unit 4, Lesson 21

like

Unit 4, Lesson 21

Unit 4, Lesson 21

DECODABLE STORIES AND SPELLING

Unit 4 • *And Away We Go!*

1. _____ days

2. _____ voyage

3. _____ wheel

4. _____ paws

5. _____ gloves

6. _____ awful

7. _____ talk

8. _____ resolved

9. _____ fondness

10. _____ moving

11. _____

_____ crowds

12. _____ driving

13. _____ calling

14. _____ news

15. _____ middle

16. _____ elephants

17. _____ crawl

18. _____ which

19. _____ sense

20. _____ recalled

Name _____ Date _____

Proofread each sentence below. Each has a Spelling word in it. Circle the Spelling word, and then write its correct spelling on the line.

1. Your mother is caling your name. _____

2. Did you hear the neews? _____

3. Ryan reecalled the events in detail. _____

4. A voyage is a long trip. _____

5. Elefants are the largest animals that live on land. _____

6. The plumber had to crawl under the sink. _____

7. I lost my glovs outside. _____

8. What is that awfull odor? _____

9. Do you know wich cup is yours? _____

10. The lion licked his paws. _____

11. Did you go and talk to Hope? _____

12. She doesn't like dealing with crouds of people. _____

13. They are drivving to Minneopolis. _____

14. I haven't seen him do his homework in dayz. _____

15. My toy car lost its weel. _____

16. I am in the midle of cleaning my room. _____

17. He felt a sence of danger when he was walking home alone. _____

18. The dog has a fondnes for playing fetch. _____

19. The problem has been resolvved. _____

20. He likes movving the furniture around. _____

Patch Stone beamed as he sat on his shiny, green   1–10
bike. He had adjusted the seat and was riding out toward   11–21
the street. He didn't ride with much speed because Goldie   22–31
was running beside him.   32–35

Patch rode the green bike past the stream and the   36–45
open prairie and onto Knob Street. He rode past a   46–55
really neat cream-colored house with flower boxes in   56–63
its windows, and then he headed down to Peanut Park.   64–73
Goldie would like to run in Peanut Park.   74–81

"Hey, Patch!" Patch didn't hear the voice call his name   82–91
at first. "Patch, over here!" Then he looked to the field   92–102
near the peach tree. It was Chuck. He and Mitch were   103–113
playing baseball for their Little League team.   114–120

Patch and Goldie went to the field to watch the game.   121–131
The boys' team beat the other team by three runs. Mitch   132–142
and Chuck were pleased to see Patch. They introduced   143–151
him to their parents. "Very nice to meet you all," said   152–162
Patch.   163–163

"Is this your dog?" asked Mitch's dad.   164–170

"That's Goldie," said Mitch to his parents. "See, he's   171–179
not mean at all. He's actually very sweet."   180–187

Mitch's dad bent to a knee to pet Goldie. "Do you want   188–199
to go for some ice cream?" Dad said. "My treat."   200–209

I read this
◯ silently.   ◯ aloud.   ◯ with a partner.   ◯ with the teacher.

Goldie ran through the park. He played in the little   1–10
pond and got all wet. Then he darted at a woman walking   11–22
on the cement path. Goldie stopped sharply, and the   23–31
woman bent to pet Goldie.   32–36
 Running in the park made Goldie tired. When Patch   37–45
Stone called him, Goldie walked to where Patch sat under   46–55
a willow tree. Goldie lay down to take a nap while Patch   56–67
talked on his cell phone.   68–72
 Goldie had a dream that he wasn't a dog anymore.   73–82
In the dream, Goldie was a man named Mark. He was a   83–94
farmer. Mark the farmer was growing celery stalks. He   95–103
sold the celery stalks from a cart for twenty-five cents   104–113
each. It was hard for Goldie to believe that he was having   114–125
a dream like this.   126–129
 Goldie woke up to find he was still in the park. Goldie 130–141
yawned as Patch patted him warmly on the back. Then   142–151
they got up and walked home from the park. Goldie   152–161
enjoyed his dream about being a celery farmer named   162–170
Mark, but he was glad to be a happy dog named Goldie.   171–182

I read this
○ silently.　　○ aloud.　　○ with a partner.　　○ with the teacher.

Unit 4 • *How Louisa Got the Right to Vote*

1. _____ dance

2. _____ cider

3. _____ heavy

4. _____ total

5. _____

   _____ weekly

6. _____ cedar

7. _____ memory

8. _____ hoping

9. _____ oboe

10. _____ fancy

11. _____ construction

12. _____ hole

13. _____ hoe

14. _____ coat

15. _____ toxic

16. _____ grew

17. _____ city

18. _____ girls

19. _____ tooth

20. _____ breath

Unit 4 • *How Louisa Got the Right to Vote*

**Proofread each sentence below. Each has a Spelling
word in it. Circle the Spelling word, and then write
its correct spelling on the line.**

1. She is wearing a fanci dress. _____

2. Our highway is under construction. _____

3. There's a hoele in my sock. _____

4. Diane was using a ho to weed the garden. _____

5. The school danse is tonight. _____

6. We were asked to buy sider at the apple orchard. ____

7. We're expecting to see heavey rain today. _____

8. His wife said she enjoys living in a big citie. _____

9. The girls will be late for his dinner. _____

10. Her toth is chipped. _____

11. I did not receive the weakly newsletter. _____

12. A cedar is a tall evergreen tree. _____

13. Melanie doesn't have any memorie of the accident. ___

14. There were toxic fumes in the air. _____

15. The flowers grew quickly. _____

16. They went out to get a breth of fresh air. _____

17. The totul is ten dollars. _____

18. We were hopping that the weather would improve. ____

19. Lindsey plays the obo. _____

20. Would you like me to hang up your coot? _____

Unit 4 • *How Louisa Got the Right to Vote* • STORY 9

While Mitch and Chuck were hiking back to Patch and	1–10
Lucy's ranch, they heard an engine. It was Mike Ginger in	11–21
his van. Mike was Patch Stone's childhood pal.	22–29
Mike stopped. "Hey, boys," said Mike Ginger. "Nice to	30–38
see you."	39–40
"Hi, Mike," they said at the same time. Then Mitch	41–50
said, "We were just shopping for a gift for Goldie."	51–60
The boys showed him the collar. "That looks like a	61–70
fine gift," Mike said. "I'm just on my way to get a gift for	71–84
my pal Patch."	85–87
"For Patch?" said Mitch. Mike explained that Goldie	88–95
and Patch share the same birthday. Then Chuck asked,	96–104
"Can we go with you? We'd like to find Patch a gift too."	105–117
Mike said that would be fine. They drove to Gina's	118–127
Bike Shop. Her shop had neat stuff! Mike wanted to get a	128–139
shiny, new bike for Patch. The price was too high for the	140–151
boys. Mike said he would pay for the bike, and they could	152–163
pay for the collar. They would say both gifts were from	164–174
all three of them.	175–178
Mike, Chuck, and Mitch drove to Patch's. They were	179–187
excited. They hoped Patch and Goldie would like their	188–196
gifts.	197–197

I read this
○ silently.   ○ aloud.   ○ with a partner.   ○ with the teacher.

Patch Stone appeared on his porch as Mitch and
Chuck arrived on his ranch with Patch's old pal Mike
Ginger.

"What's this all about?" Patch said to the boys. "Where
did you find this old walnut?" Patch was talking about
Mike.

"Why did you call him a walnut?" asked Mitch.

"I've known Mike for as long as I can recall," said
Patch. "That's just a silly, little nickname I call him
because he never cracks up at my jokes."

"Well, the boys are exhausted from the walk to town,"
said Mike Ginger to Patch. "Get out that grill, and let's
cook up some sausage. We're starving."

Patch smiled as he disappeared to get the grill. He
returned several moments later with the grill and Goldie.
Mike Ginger and the boys gave Patch and Goldie their
birthday gifts. Patch liked the bike as much as Goldie
liked his new collar. During dinner, Mike and Patch
talked about old times when they hauled fuel all over the
United States.

1–9
10–19
20–20
21–30
31–40
41–41
42–50
51–61
62–71
72–79
80–89
90–100
101–106
107–116
117–125
126–135
136–145
146–154
155–165
166–167

I read this
○ silently.   ○ aloud.   ○ with a partner.   ○ with the teacher.

DECODABLE STORIES AND SPELLING

Unit 4 • *How Louisa Got the Right to Vote*

Cut out the boxes on this page to make your own
set of Sight Word cards. The following Sight Words
are reviewed in this lesson.

her Unit 4, Lesson 16	**was** Unit 4, Lesson 16
his Unit 4, Lesson 16	**were** Unit 4, Lesson 16
said Unit 4, Lesson 16	 Unit 4, Lesson 16
see Unit 4, Lesson 16	 Unit 4, Lesson 16

Unit 4 • *Fighting for Equality*

Cut out the boxes on this page to make your own
set of Sight Word cards. The following Sight Words
are reviewed in this lesson.

any Unit 4, Lesson 26	**never** Unit 4, Lesson 26
been Unit 4, Lesson 26	**with** Unit 4, Lesson 26
for Unit 4, Lesson 26	 Unit 4, Lesson 26
from Unit 4, Lesson 26	 Unit 4, Lesson 26

Unit 4 • *Fighting for Equality*

1. _____ pages

2. _____ six

3. _____ hyena

4. _____ spry

5. _____ hyphen

6. _____ files

7. _____ exceptional

8. _____ historic

9. _____ cry

10. _____ critical

11. _____ plunge

12. _____ think

13. _____ student

14. _____ cyclone

15. _____ thighs

16. _____ spring

17. _____ July

18. _____ biology

19. _____ wise

20. _____ majestic

Name _____ Date _____

Unit 4 • *Fighting for Equality*

Proofread each sentence below. Each has a Spelling word in it. Circle the Spelling word, and then write its correct spelling on the line.

1. The spri woman walks two miles every day for excercise. _____

2. Your sentence is missing a hiphen. _____

3. My birthday is in July. _____

4. We have a biologe test today along with math. _____

5. You never make a wize decision. _____

6. The show starts at siks o'clock. _____

7. I didn't plunje into the water. _____

8. I thinc I will go to bed. _____

9. The thies are from the top part of the leg down to the knee. _____

10. Last spring, we traveled to New Mexico. _____

11. This book has some pages missing. _____

12. A hyena looks like a dog. _____

13. Do you have any of the fils? _____

14. The company's president must make a criticil decision. _____

15. She hung the majestuc portrait on the wall. _____

16. The ciclone caused a lot of damage. _____

17. The signing of the peace treaty was an historac moment. _____

18. Rachel's performance in the play was exceptionul. _____

19. He's going to crie when you leave. _____

20. Miss Amy has been a student teacher. _____

Patch Stone called Mitch and Chuck over to his   1–9
yellow house. He had some news to tell the boys.   10–19

"Men," he said to them, "I've just sold my ranch, and   20–30
I'm going to move to the coast."   31–37

"You're leaving?" said Mitch sadly. "We'll never see   38–45
you anymore?"   46–47

"I'll be leaving as soon as they have my boat ready,"   48–58
said Patch. "I had a boat made so I could sail around   59–70
Earth."   71–71

"Is Goldie going with you?" asked Chuck.   72–78

"I'm afraid so," said Patch. "Goldie will go wherever I   79–88
go."   89–89

Mitch and Chuck told Patch that they would miss him   90–99
and Goldie. Then Patch spoke, "You can visit me on the   100–110
coast. It's only a short drive, and your parents can take   111–121
you there. You might even come for a ride on the boat!"   122–133

"So who owns the ranch now?" asked Mitch.   134–141

"I sold it to Mike Ginger and his wife, Rose," Patch   142–152
told them. "So you can still come over and play."   153–162

Mitch and Chuck told Patch that they were sad he was   163–173
leaving, but they looked forward to seeing his boat.   174–182

I read this
○ silently.   ○ aloud.   ○ with a partner.   ○ with the teacher.

It was mid-July. Mitch and Chuck were hanging out	1–9
with Mike and Rose Ginger on the ranch. At noon, when	10–20
the mail came, there was a postcard from Patch Stone.	21–30
"Look," said Rose, "we've received word from Patch!"	31–38
Rose read the whole thing out loud. It read:	39–47

Dear Mike, Rose, Mitch, Chuck, and all who read this,	48–57
I truly hope you are all well. Things on the boat are	58–69
going smoothly. It's nice to sail at night under the bright	70–80
moon. I named my boat Lucy, after my sister. I've been	81–91
sailing on Lucy for a long time. I have a lot of free time,	92–105
so I sing songs, and I learned how to play the tuba.	106–117
Goldie likes it out here, but he misses all of you. I	118–129
don't think he likes my tuba playing.	130–136
When I was fishing for food on the roof of my boat, I	137–149
caught a tuna! It was huge. That's the truth. I'll tell more	150–161
about this later.	162–164
I'll be back near Cherryville shortly—at the end of	165–174
July. Mike, I hope you haven't ruined my ranch. I'll see	175–185
you all soon.	186–188

Yours truly,	189–190
Patch & Goldie	191–193

Mike, Rose, Mitch, and Chuck were happy to hear	194–202
from Patch. It sounded as if things were going well. Mitch	203–213
and Chuck were glad they would be able to see Patch	214–224
and Goldie soon.	225–227

I read this
○ silently.   ○ aloud.   ○ with a partner.   ○ with the teacher.

Name _____ Date _____

Unit 5 • *A Tour of Hawaii's Volcanoes*

1. _____ _____ jacket

2. _____ _____ restored

3. _____ _____ notch

4. _____ _____ splurged

5. _____ _____ orange

6. _____ _____ garage

7. _____ ditch

8. _____ bragging

9. _____ generations

10. _____ motor

11. _____ sight

12. _____ radiator

13. _____ while

14. _____ core

15. _____ game

16. _____ variety

17. _____ before

18. _____ twilight

19. _____ submarine

20. _____ idea

Name _____ Date _____

Unit 5 • *A Tour of Hawaii's Volcanoes*

Proofread each sentence below. Each has a Spelling word in it. Circle the Spelling word, and then write its correct spelling on the line.

1. Do you have an idea for Tina's birthday gift? _____

2. The radiator in her car does need a replacement. _____

3. How could Vicky read her book while she waited? _____

4. Do you think this noch on the table can be repaired? _____

5. Justin splurjed and bought a new car. _____

6. She is bragging about her new house. _____

7. The Miller family has lived in town for many jenerations. _____

8. A dust jacet is used to protect hardcover books. _____

9. After a few days of rest, his health was restorred. _____

10. We made a varity of cookies for the bake sale. _____

11. Wash your hands befor dinner. _____

12. My bicycle is in the garaje. _____

13. The snow-capped mountains are a beautiful site. _____

14. Dusk is sometimes called twilite. _____

15. Look at the water that has collected in the dich. _____

16. We took a tour of the submarine while we were on vacation. _____

17. I had oatmeal and an oranj for breakfast. _____

18. The boat's moter needs to be repaired. _____

19. The inner coar of the earth is composed of iron. _____

20. Checkers is my favorite gam. _____

Unit 5 • *A Tour of Hawaii's Volcanoes* • STORY 1

Late at night, my brother and I would lie in our beds	1–12
and speculate about what we would do when we grew	13–22
up. My favorite idea was always the same: to take a trip	23–34
around the world.	35–37
I would tell my brother how I would first ride the rails	38–49
on a train and head out of our state. Then I would hop a	50–63
plane to the coast. There I would catch a freighter and	64–74
sail south across the equator. I had other travel aims, too,	75–85
like riding a sleigh across wide fields of winter snow or	86–96
bouncing on a camel over burning desert trails.	97–104
As I have aged, I have been able to do most of those	105–117
things. But my brother has really been around the world.	118–127
Today is a space shuttle pilot. From way up in space	128–138
he has circled the globe. Many times he has flown the	139–149
shuttle as it has traced a path around the curve of our	150–161
globe. On his third flight, he even flew over our old	162–172
neighborhood.	173–173
When we were kids, we dreamed big things, and our	174–183
dreams came true! Where does your biggest dream take	184–192
you?	193–193

I read this
○ silently.   ○ aloud.   ○ with a partner.   ○ with the teacher.

"Those paw prints had me scratching my head," said Ranger Dawn Jones.

"Why?" asked Tommy Chatter, a Channel Five TV reporter. He held a microphone right under the tall ranger's jaw.

"Because the paws had three claws and the prints suggested an animal that walked like a person. Join me for a look," said Ranger Jones. As she talked, the Channel Five camera showed paw prints circled in chalk.

"Couldn't you match those prints to something?" asked Tommy.

"We did, and we caught the person who made them," explained the ranger.

"A person?" asked the reporter.

"Yes," grinned the ranger. "By chance, I was in a costume shop and saw a costume with a big paw and claws that looked much like the prints. And then I had a hunch."

"What?" asked Tommy Chatter.

"I remembered that my boy had a costume like that," said Ranger Jones.

Tommy Chatter was so surprised he almost hit his chin with the microphone. "Your son made the paw prints!" he exclaimed.

"He and a few pals did," said Ranger Jones.

Tommy Chatter turned to the camera and said, "I think the paw print case is closed!"

1–9
10–12
13–20
21–29
30–31
32–40
41–50
51–61
62–69
70–76
77–78
79–88
89–91
92–96
97–106
107–117
118–129
130–130
131–134
135–144
145–147
148–156
157–165
166–168
169–177
178–186
187–193

I read this
○ silently.   ○ aloud.   ○ with a partner.   ○ with the teacher.

Unit 5 • *A Tour of Hawaii's Volcanoes*

Cut out the boxes on this page to make your own set of Sight Word cards. The following Sight Words are reviewed in this lesson.

does

Unit 5, Lesson 1

Unit 5, Lesson 1

look

Unit 5, Lesson 1

Unit 5, Lesson 1

how

Unit 5, Lesson 1

Unit 5, Lesson 1

many

Unit 5, Lesson 1

Unit 5, Lesson 1

Unit 5 • *California on the Move: Earthquakes*

Cut out the boxes on this page to make your own
set of Sight Word cards. The following Sight Words
are reviewed in this lesson.

often Unit 5, Lesson 6	Unit 5, Lesson 6
once Unit 5, Lesson 6	Unit 5, Lesson 6
some Unit 5, Lesson 6	Unit 5, Lesson 6
want Unit 5, Lesson 6	Unit 5, Lesson 6

DECODABLE STORIES AND SPELLING

Name _____ Date _____

Unit 5 • *California on the Move: Earthquakes*

1. _____ faint

2. _____ squirrels

3. _____ moisture

4. _____

_____ equal

5. _____ attractive

6. _____ claims

7. _____ quickly

8. _____ birthday

9. _____ after

10. _____ weighs

11. _____ pain

12. _____ when

13. _____ voice

14. _____ world

15. _____ clay

16. _____ semicircle

17. _____ annoy

18. _____ positive

19. _____ clerk

20. _____ women

Unit 5 • *California on the Move: Earthquakes*

Proofread each sentence below. Each has a Spelling word in it. Circle the Spelling word, and then write its correct spelling on the line.

1. The law clurk performed research for the judge often. _____

2. The baby ways ten pounds. _____

3. I have some pan in my arm. _____

4. Hayley is very attractave. _____

5. Adam clams to be the best soccer player on the team. _____

6. There are seven continents in the werld. _____

7. Bricks are made of clai. _____

8. The faint noise is coming from the basement. _____

9. The squirrels are burying nuts for the winter. _____

10. For once I didn't mean to annoi you. _____

11. She has a positeve outlook. _____

12. Her birthday is on Friday. _____

13. We want to watch a movie aftar dinner. _____

14. She has a beautiful singing voyce. _____

15. She did not think that her school work was ekual to her abilities. _____

16. Moysture falls from clouds in the form of rain. _____

17. Reese walked kuickly home. _____

18. When it rains, it pours. _____

19. A cemicircle is a half circle. _____

20. Five women walked into the store. _____

Tommy Chatter chewed his pencil and looked at a   1–9
tiny, flashing light high in the night sky. The light headed   10–20
toward him and got brighter. He stuck the pencil inside   21–30
his TV reporter's vest and grabbed his cell phone. He   31–40
called his supervisor, Cindy Brown.   41–45

"Cindy," said Tommy when she answered, "Do you   46–53
want to hear some exciting news? I'm on the Stacy City   54–64
skyscraper, and I see a bright, white light flashing in the   65–75
sky. I think it's a spaceship from another planet."   76–84

"That's not likely," said Cindy. She often said this to   85–94
Tommy.   95–95

"It's getting closer," said Tommy in an excited voice.   96–104
"I'll have a big news story once I spy a real spaceship!"   105–116

"That's not likely," said Cindy. "Try to describe what   117–125
you see."   126–127

"It's wide and has lights on three sides. It's making a   128–138
strange sound," said Tommy.   139–142

"Tommy, I think . . ." Cindy tried to say, but Tommy   143–154
stopped her.   155–156

"I see writing on the spaceship," he yelled into the   157–166
phone. "I see a big number five!"   167–173

"That's likely," sighed Cindy, "because I sent the   174–181
Channel Five News helicopter to pick you up on the   182–191
Stacy City skyscraper."   192–194

"Oh," said Tommy. "Never mind about my big news   195–203
story."   204–204

I read this
○ silently.   ○ aloud.   ○ with a partner.   ○ with the teacher.

On Channel Five TV News, Jen Gentry was reporting — 1–9
that voters would have a tough choice in the July — 10–19
election, when she stopped and read a piece of paper. — 20–29
"This just in," she said. "We have a major story in Ridge — 30–41
Point. We are joining our reporter Tommy Chatter. He has — 42–51
the details." — 52–53

Tommy Chatter's face was now on the screen. "Jen, — 54–62
I am standing in the village of Ridge Point," Tommy said — 63–73
into his microphone. "I have discovered oil in the soil — 74–83
here." — 84–84

"Oil in Ridge Point?" asked Jen. — 85–90

"Yes, there is a giant pool of oil behind me," said — 91–101
Tommy. The camera showed a moist, oily spot on the soil — 102–112
by the street. — 113–115

"Tommy," said Jen, who was looking at a TV monitor, — 116–125
"I see that also behind you is a tow truck with a wrecked — 126–138
van on its hook." — 139–142

"Yes," said Tommy as he turned around. — 143–149

"And the van seems to be leaking oil," added Jen. — 150–159

"Yes," said Tommy. Then he paused and said, "I am — 160–169
sorry to disappoint you, Jen. But oil has not been — 170–179
discovered in Ridge Point. Back to you, Jen." — 180–187

I read this
○ silently.   ○ aloud.   ○ with a partner.   ○ with the teacher.

Unit 5 • *Yellowstone National Park: Nature's "Hotspot"*

1. _____ bicycle

2. _____ sighed

3. _____ science

4. _____ sky

5. _____ once

6. _____ arrangements

7. _____ graphic

8. _____ race

9. _____ ginger

10. _____ style

11. _____ large

12. _____ right

13. _____ wrench

14. _____ phone

15. _____ decide

16. _____ magically

17. _____ flight

18. _____ reply

19. _____ judgment

20. _____ disagree

Name _____ Date _____

Unit 5 • *Yellowstone National Park: Nature's "Hotspot"*

Proofread each sentence below. Each has a Spelling word in it. Circle the Spelling word, and then write its correct spelling on the line.

1. She exercised poor judjment. _____

2. Harry might dissagree with you again. _____

3. Dark clouds moved across the skie. _____

4. Onse in a while, we go to the museum during the school year. _____

5. Did you wrench your ankle when you fell? _____

6. Carla, answer the fone. _____

7. He sied because he missed his friends. _____

8. Sience is the study of the physical world. _____

9. She majically appeared in front of me. _____

10. Did you have a nice flite? _____

11. Leo gave a graphic description of the accident. _____

12. If you decide to come to the party, let me know. _____

13. Glenn rode his bicicle to school once this year. _____

14. Who is in charge of the travel arrangements? _____

15. The recipe calls for a half a teaspoon of jinger. _____

16. He is rite-handed. _____

17. Who won the rase? _____

18. I like her stile of decorating. _____

19. Jake did not replie to my question. _____

20. There's a larje pond on the property. _____

Late in the evening, Tommy Chatter sat in the Channel   1–10

Five TV van. It was a quiet night. He was waiting for the   11–23

biggest news story of the year to happen. "I am hungry.   24–34

I need something to eat," he said to himself. "I feel like   35–46

ordering a sandwich."   47–49

He zipped the van over to Zack's Snack Shop. At the   50–60

drive-up window, he leaned out and said to Zack, "A   61–70

sandwich, please."   71–72

"Yes, sir," said Zack. "What size do you require?"   73–81

"Medium, please," Tommy said.   82–85

"With zesty cheese?" Zack asked.   86–90

"Yes, and green peppers," he said.   91–96

"Any extra seasonings?" asked Zack.   97–101

"Let me see," Tommy said slowly. Just then his cell   102–111

phone rang.   112–113

"Sorry," he said to Zack. "I need to answer this. It   114–124

means my supervisor needs me again!"   125–130

Then he said into the cell phone, "Hello!"   131–138

"It's me," said Cindy Brown. "Quit talking, and turn   139–147

your microphone off."   148–150

"Oh, no!" screamed Tommy. He looked at the   151–158

microphone switch. It was on. He quickly flipped it off.   159–168

"On the TV news, the whole city just heard you order   169–179

a sandwich!" said Cindy.   180–183

I read this
◯ silently.   ◯ aloud.   ◯ with a partner.   ◯ with the teacher.

Unit 5 • *Yellowstone National Park: Nature's "Hotspot"* • STORY 6

Tommy Chatter spoke to a class about being a	1–9
reporter.	10–10
"Mr. Chatter," said a student, "you are a person who	11–20
has worked all over the world. What's the worst thing you	21–31
ever saw?"	32–33
"Well, I was driving the yellow Channel Five News	34–42
van from Texas to New Mexico," said Tommy. "Suddenly,	43–51
I heard something explode. I felt a wave of horror and	52–62
yanked the van into a yard on the side of the road."	63–74
"What happened next?" asked the student.	75–80
"Afterward, I turned the motor off and got out of the	81–91
van. Then I saw it," said Tommy.	92–98
"This is exciting!" exclaimed the student. "What did	99–106
you see?"	107–108
"A flat tire," said Tommy. "I had a blow out. I was	109–120
filled with terror."	121–123
"Why?" the student asked.	124–127
"I knew I didn't have an extra tire, so I couldn't fix the	128–140
flat. I also knew I would have to walk about six miles to	141–153
the next town," explained Tommy.	154–158
The student was disappointed. She didn't expect such	159–166
a dull story.	167–169

I read this
○ silently.   ○ aloud.   ○ with a partner.   ○ with the teacher.

DECODABLE STORIES AND SPELLING

Unit 5 • *Yellowstone National Park: Nature's "Hotspot"*

Cut out the boxes on this page to make your own set of Sight Word cards. The following Sight Words are reviewed in this lesson.

# again	
Unit 5, Lesson 11	Unit 5, Lesson 11
# answer	
Unit 5, Lesson 11	Unit 5, Lesson 11
# who	
Unit 5, Lesson 11	Unit 5, Lesson 11
# year	
Unit 5, Lesson 11	Unit 5, Lesson 11

Unit 5 • *Frozen Earth Movers*

Cut out the boxes on this page to make your own
set of Sight Word cards. The following Sight Words
are reviewed in this lesson.

enough

Unit 5, Lesson 16

Unit 5, Lesson 16

give

Unit 5, Lesson 16

Unit 5, Lesson 16

these

Unit 5, Lesson 16

Unit 5, Lesson 16

where

Unit 5, Lesson 16

Unit 5, Lesson 16

DECODABLE STORIES AND SPELLING

Unit 5 • *Frozen Earth Movers*

1. _____ terrible

2. _____ need

3. _____ vinegar

4. _____ read

5. _____ zipper

6. _____ generous

7. _____ nurse

8. _____ sugar

9. _____ terrain

10. _____ count

11. _____ beet

12. _____

 _____ generate

13. _____ hurry

14. _____ stream

15. _____ fled

16. _____ quickly

17. _____ surprise

18. _____ sour

19. _____ frozen

20. _____ beat

Name _____ Date _____

Unit 5 • *Frozen Earth Movers*

Proofread each sentence below. Each has a Spelling word in it. Circle the Spelling word, and then write its correct spelling on the line.

1. Would you like sugar in your tea? _____

2. Will you hury up and give me an answer? _____

3. Shannon had a sower look on her face. _____

4. The nerse gave me some medicine. _____

5. Where did she genarate copies of the flyer? _____

6. I have a terible headache. _____

7. I've already red these books. _____

8. Who would like to beatt on the African drum? _____

9. The man fled the scene quickly. _____

10. There is enough vineger to make salad dressing. _____

11. You can cownt on me. _____

12. The flowers were a nice serprise for my birthday this year. _____

13. We need to get milk and fruit at the store. _____

14. The ziper on her pants is broken. _____

15. She quickley blamed her brother. _____

16. My hands are frozen. _____

17. She gave me a jenerous amount of ice cream. _____

18. The rugged terrain is hard to walk on. _____

19. My mother made beett salad again. _____

20. A streem runs through the park. _____

"This is Tommy Chatter from Channel Five TV News   1–9
reporting from the Wren Museum. Today the museum   10–17
opened a new display of old bowls, jars, and pots,"   18–27
reported Tommy, holding a microphone. "I am speaking   28–35
with Professor Wren himself about the display.   36–42

"Hello, professor. Give us the facts about this display.   43–51
These large bowls are interesting," said Tommy. He   52–59
pointed to the yellow bowl that had dark gold trim. It had   60–71
figures painted on it.   72–75

"Yes," agreed Professor Wren. "The art on it helps us   76–85
know what life was like thousands of years ago. On this   86–96
side, we see an old farm and garden tools. This looks like   97–108
a wooden wrench, and this is a stone hammer." He was   109–119
pointing to things on the bowl.   120–125

"You would need a strong arm and wrist to use a stone   126–137
hammer," said Tommy.   138–140

"Yes, I suppose," said Professor Wren. "This side   141–148
shows a whole family in a yard in the morning."   149–158

"If I'm not wrong, I know how this large bowl was   159–169
used," said Tommy.   170–172

"You do?" asked Professor Wren.   173–177

"Yes," said Tommy. "The family rose with the sun and   178–187
filled the bowl with cereal."   188–192

The professor said, "That is enough, Mr. Chatter; this   193–201
is not a joke."   202–205

"Sorry," said Tommy.   206–208

I read this
○ silently.   ○ aloud.   ○ with a partner.   ○ with the teacher.

Cindy Brown, the head of Channel Five TV News, was	1–10
at her desk. She phoned Tommy Chatter at his home.	11–20
"Tommy, I need you to check a report that a crook took	21–32
three books from the library."	33–37
"What books?" asked Tommy. "Where could the books	38–45
be?"	46–46
"The first is called *Cooking for Camp*. It tells how	47–56
to bake things like banana bread and carrot cake," said	57–66
Cindy.	67–67
"I just read it," said Tommy.	68–73
"The next book is about a local kid who plays soccer.	74–84
It's called *The Rookie's Foot*," said Cindy.	85–91
"I just read that too!" said Tommy.	92–98
"The third has a heavy leather cover. It's a book of	99–109
poems called *In Pleasant Meadows*," said Cindy.	110–116
"Wow! I just read that too," said Tommy. Then	117–125
with dread in his voice, he added, "Let me look at my	126–137
bookshelves, Cindy."	138–139
Cindy heard his footsteps as Tommy ran to check his	140–149
shelves. In seconds, he was back.	150–155
"I solved the case," said Tommy. "I have the books.	156–165
They were due at the library last week."	166–173
"I know," chuckled Cindy. "The library called here to	174–182
ask you to bring them back." Then she hung up.	183–192

I read this
○ silently.   ○ aloud.   ○ with a partner.   ○ with the teacher.

Name _____ Date _____

1. _____ _____   dirty

2. _____ _____   carnival

3. _____ __

   _____ .   preschool

4. _____ ___   cook

5. _____ ___   harmless

6. _____ ___   below

7. _____ ___   artist

8. _____ ___   explosion

9. _____ ___   knit

10. _____ ___   bird

11. _____ ___   slowing

12. _____ ___   wool

13. _____ ___   knee

14. _____ ___   pole

15. _____ ___   opening

16. _____ ___   start

17. _____ ___   going

18. _____ ___   preheat

19. _____ ___   hopeless

20. _____ ___   confirm

Unit 5 • *Cutting Through the Layers of Time*

Proofread each sentence below. Each has a Spelling word in it. Circle the Spelling word, and then write its correct spelling on the line.

1. There are enough crackers on the shelf beloow the flour. _____

2. She thinks she is hopeles at geometry. _____

3. This company is a great tight-nit organization. _____

4. There's an opeening in the trees. _____

5. There were a lot of rides at the carrnival. _____

6. I have banged my kne on the table. _____

7. Preheet the oven to 400 degrees. _____

8. Cook the garlic for one minute to give the food more flavor. _____

9. They did not confirm or deny the rumor. _____

10. The exploosion of the fireworks scared the dog. _____

11. Where are we gooing to buy clothes for the trip? _____

12. I put the derty clothes in the washing machine. _____

13. Kelly is going to preeschool tomorrow morning. _____

14. These whale sharks are giant harmless sharks. _____

15. The aartist painted a seascape. _____

16. The bird flew out of its cage. _____

17. The wol blanket is in the chest. _____

18. The car hit the telephone pol. _____

19. The show is about to start, so I need my eye glasses. _____

20. The traffic is slowwing. _____

Unit 5 • *Cutting Through the Layers of Time* • Story 9

Did you ever train a dog? It's not an easy job. Mom	1–12
has explained to me that in some ways it's like raising a	13–24
baby.	25–25
Wiggles was just eight weeks old when he came to our	26–36
house. We received good advice from our vet. "Training a	37–46
dog is hard work. You can't buy your way around it. The	47–58
main thing is to be kind."	59–64
We take Wiggles out in the neighborhood every	65–72
chance we get. Mom, Dad, Gus, and I take turns. When it	73–84
rains, Wiggles still gets to go out. I slip on a raincoat and	85–97
galoshes and we play in the puddles.	98–104
After lots of training, Wiggles is able to understand us.	105–114
When we say *stop*, Wiggles waits at the gate. When we	115–125
say *go*, he races away.	126–130
Wiggles helps me too. Last Friday, when I was tired	131–140
and sad after a big test, he came running to meet me at	141–153
the gate, wagging his tail. As soon as he caught my eye,	154–165
he changed my mood from sad to happy!	166–173

I read this
○ silently.   ○ aloud.   ○ with a partner.   ○ with the teacher.

Unit 5 • *Cutting Through the Layers of Time* • STORY 10

I am so proud of my city. I delight in walking	1–11
downtown and taking in the sights, smells, and sounds.	12–20
Outside city hall, a fountain spouts a splashing gusher	21–29
that catches light in the sunshine. It is surrounded by	30–39
flower gardens in bloom. In fact, there are thousands of	40–49
flowers all over downtown.	50–53
The shops around city hall all have brightly colored	54–62
awnings and windows. Behind Brown's Book and Bakery	63–70
Shop I found a little patio. You order food there. They	71–81
have great fish chowder and fresh bread.	82–88
South of the shops is a park with a stage. Large	89–99
crowds gather for concerts and to watch agile dancers.	100–108
The sound of music fills the whole park for hours.	109–118
You can ride the free yellow trolley around town. I	119–128
like to relax on the upper level of the trolley and look at	129–141
all I can. I am not in a rush. I can spend large amounts of	142–156
time enjoying my hometown.	157–160

I read this
○ silently.   ○ aloud.   ○ with a partner.   ○ with the teacher.

DECODABLE STORIES AND SPELLING

Name _____ Date _____

Cut out the boxes on this page to make your own set of Sight Word cards. The following Sight Words are reviewed in this lesson.

buy

Unit 5, Lesson 21

Unit 5, Lesson 21

eye

Unit 5, Lesson 21

Unit 5, Lesson 21

have

Unit 5, Lesson 21

Unit 5, Lesson 21

great

Unit 5, Lesson 21

Unit 5, Lesson 21

Unit 5 • *How a Cave Is Formed*

Cut out the boxes on this page to make your own
set of Sight Word cards. The following Sight Words
are reviewed in this lesson.

color

Unit 5, Lesson 26

Unit 5, Lesson 26

come

Unit 5, Lesson 26

Unit 5, Lesson 26

door

Unit 5, Lesson 26

Unit 5, Lesson 26

learn

Unit 5, Lesson 26

Unit 5, Lesson 26

Name _____ Date _____

Unit 5 • *How a Cave Is Formed*

1. _____ subject

2. _____ excited

3. _____ icy

4. _____ tax

5. _____ peach

6. _____ watch

7. _____ repeat

8. _____ field

9. _____ gigantic

10. _____ chilly

11. _____ improvement

12. _____ attached

13. _____ windy

14. _____ even

15. _____ belong

16. _____ van

17. _____ relax

18. _____ catch

19. _____ achievement

20. _____ relieve

Name _____ Date _____

Unit 5 • *How a Cave Is Formed*

Proofread each sentence below. Each has a Spelling word in it. Circle the Spelling word, and then write its correct spelling on the line.

1. Is it chilly in here? _____

2. The school vann drove us to the museum to learn about dinosaurs. _____

3. What is the color of the peech you have? _____

4. Let's play cach. _____

5. What is the subject of your report? _____

6. Our car slid on the icey road. _____

7. Finishing the marathon was an achevement. _____

8. Does your hat beelong on the floor? _____

9. They began to taks my nerves. _____

10. Someday, I would like to work in the feld of medicine. _____

11. I wish I could relieve her pain. _____

12. Please don't repeet what I said to anyone else. _____

13. The sticker is attatched to the wall by the door. _____

14. She is very exxcited about the great news. _____

15. Did you come and wach him play basketball? _____

16. Your bedroom is a jigantic mess. _____

17. The company made an improvemnt to their product. _____

18. Chicago is known as the "windie city." _____

19. It will be great to relax and read a book. _____

20. The pictures on the wall are not even. _____

Name _____   Date _____

The big pitcher thought he was cool. I studied him as	1–11
he threw a few warm-up pitches. He had an attitude. He	12–22
was smooth, and he knew he could pitch well.	23–31
It was true that he was good, but I think I'm a good	32–44
athlete too. My job was to use a bat to hit what the big	45–58
pitcher threw.	59–60
I stepped to the plate. The big pitcher threw the first	61–71
pitch. I could see it come at me fast. Then it blew past	72–84
me. Whew! That was fast! I stepped back and drew in a	85–96
breath. I gathered my thoughts and my strength. "I can	97–106
hit this pitch," I told myself.	107–112
I stepped back into the batter's box. I was loose and	113–123
ready. The big pitcher held the ball next to the blue-	124–134
colored numeral on his shirt. Then he wound up and	135–144
threw again. This time I swung. Boom! I cranked the ball.	145–155
It zoomed up and over the pitcher's head. It flew out of	156–167
the park but near the foul pole.	168–174
The chief of the umpiring crew raised his finger and	175–184
waved it in a circle. He ruled it a home run!	185–195

I read this
○ silently.   ○ aloud.   ○ with a partner.   ○ with the teacher.

Unit 5 • *How a Cave Is Formed* • STORY 12

Rabbit asked Turtle, "How can such little legs get you	1–10
places?"	11–11
Turtle shrugged and said, "Big deal. I've got short	12–20
legs. So what! Let's run a race and see who wins."	21–31
Rabbit gave Turtle a strange look. "You must be	32–40
joking. But okay, a race would be fun. First runner to the	41–52
bridge wins."	53–54
Rabbit jumped up and jetted up the path. He left	55–64
Turtle in the dust.	65–68
After a few seconds, Rabbit looked back. "I can stop	69–78
and grab a snack," Rabbit panted. "Turtle is still far	79–88
back."	89–89
Rabbit munched on vegetables until he wasn't hungry.	90–97
Turtle was still far behind him. "I'm in no danger of	98–108
losing. I have an open door to an easy win! I'll just take	109–121
a quick nap," Rabbit said. He rubbed his face and napped	122–132
on the gentle grass by a large stump.	133–140
When Rabbit woke from his nap, he stretched his legs	141–150
and looked around. Turtle wasn't in sight. Rabbit hopped	151–159
up and ran to the bridge, snickering at how far ahead of	160–171
the Turtle he was.	172–175
When Rabbit got to the bridge, Turtle was sitting	176–184
under it. Rabbit was stunned. Turtle had beaten him!	185–193
"Enjoy your nap?" asked Turtle. "My little legs didn't	194–202
stop running. I jogged by you as you gently snored in the	203–214
sun."	215–215
Do you think Rabbit learned his lesson?	216–222

I read this
○ silently.   ○ aloud.   ○ with a partner.   ○ with the teacher.

Name _____ Date _____

Unit 6 • *Sounds of Moonlight*

1. _____ disobey

2. _____ blew

3. _____ true

4. _____ prehistoric

5. _____ school

6. _____ wrong

7. _____ tear

8. _____ rules

9. _____ shells

10. _____ tutor

11. _____ drinking

12. _____ blue

13. _____ ring

14. _____ flute

15. _____ improvements

16. _____ spread

17. _____ ruby

18. _____ fish

19. _____ timeless

20. _____ native

Name _____ Date _____

Unit 6 • *Sounds of Moonlight*

Proofread each sentence below. Each has a Spelling word in it. Circle the Spelling word, and then write its correct spelling on the line.

1. Would these trees be nateve to the area? _____

2. You should know the ruls of the game. _____

3. Preehistoric time is the period before written history. _____

4. Your roby necklace is beautiful. _____

5. He blew out all of his birthday candles. _____

6. They are drinnking tea. _____

7. Come to the beach and collect shells with me. _____

8. I'm going to Claire's house after schol. _____

9. I left my rinng on the table. _____

10. There's a tare in my shirt. _____

11. This book is timeless. _____

12. Jeff's totor helped him improve his writing. _____

13. The home improvemnts could increase the value of the house.

_____

14. Her car is the color blew. _____

15. The name of my fissh is Sam. _____

16. If you dissobey, you will get in trouble. _____

17. The movie is based on a trew story. _____

18. We took a wrong turn after we came in the door. _____

19. Jordan is taking flote lessons. _____

20. Her rash spread quickly. _____

It wasn't an exciting race. After fifteen laps around	1–9
the track, race car driver Mark Shield was far ahead. He	10–20
had led from the start of the thirty-three-lap race.	21–29
"We have a good lead," Mark yelled over the two-way	30–39
radio to his crew chief, Sparky Meter.	40–46
"I believe you're right, Mark," Sparky yelled back, "but	47–55
you would be smart to stay alert. You don't want to be	56–67
taken by surprise."	68–70
After another fifteen laps, Mark was still in the lead,	71–80
but a dark green car had almost caught up with him. With	81–92
just three laps to go, Mark was suddenly in a real race!	93–104
"Mark," Sparky called into the radio, "your lead isn't	105–113
very large now. You should speed up and keep your	114–123
hands on the wheel."	124–127
Suddenly the green car was next to Mark. Although	128–136
the finish line wasn't far, Mark was hot and tired. He	137–147
could barely feel his foot on the gas pedal, but he pushed	148–159
it harder. He felt a slight increase in his speed. Was it	160–171
enough? His car shot out a bit and crossed the finish line	172–183
just three feet ahead of the green car.	184–191
The crowd cheered as Mark parked his car. He stood	192–201
between Sparky and the car as he received his trophy	202–211
with glee and relief.	212–215

I read this
◯ silently.   ◯ aloud.   ◯ with a partner.   ◯ with the teacher.

Unit 6 • *Sounds of Moonlight* • STORY 2

Sam was riding his bike to Max's house. Max had a   1–11
broken swing, and Sam was going to try to fix it. Sam   12–23
had a knack for fixing things.   24–29

As Sam was pedaling to Max's house, he heard a   30–39
knocking and knew that something was wrong with his   40–48
bike. Because Sam had his toolbox with him, he decided   49–58
to fix it right away.   59–63

Sam knelt down to take a look at the bike. The chain   64–75
was half off! Sam tapped here and he tapped there. With   76–86
a few strong adjustments, Sam was able to place the   87–96
chain back. Sam wanted to relax, but he still had to ride   97–108
six blocks to Max's.   109–112

At Max's, it didn't take Sam too much toil to see that a   113–125
spring in the swing was missing. Sam had an extra spring   126–136
in his toolbox and soon Max's swing was back to normal.   137–147

Next Sam rode back home. As he pedaled, he thought,   148–157
"If stuff needs fixing, I'm the man to call! I know I can fix   158–171
everything!"   172–172

Just then, Sam heard a knocking in his bike again.   173–182
The chain fell off. Sam stopped and thought, "Well, almost   183–192
everything!"   193–193

I read this
○ silently.   ○ aloud.   ○ with a partner.   ○ with the teacher.

Unit 6 • *Sounds of Moonlight*

Cut out the boxes on this page to make your own
set of Sight Word cards. The following Sight Words
are reviewed in this lesson.

could	
Unit 6, Lesson 1	Unit 6, Lesson 1
should	
Unit 6, Lesson 1	Unit 6, Lesson 1
would	
Unit 6, Lesson 1	Unit 6, Lesson 1

Name _____ Date _____

Unit 6 • *Alice the Artist*

Cut out the boxes on this page to make your own
set of Sight Word cards. The following Sight Words
are reviewed in this lesson.

earn	
Unit 6, Lesson 6	Unit 6, Lesson 6
move	
Unit 6, Lesson 6	Unit 6, Lesson 6
other	
Unit 6, Lesson 6	Unit 6, Lesson 6
Unit 6, Lesson 6	Unit 6, Lesson 6

Unit 6 • *Alice the Artist*

1. _____ thrifty

2. _____ fallen

3. _____ try

4. _____ wipe

5. _____ bath

6. _____ wall

7. _____ idea

8. _____

   _____ disappointed

9. _____ deny

10. _____ taught

11. _____ light

12. _____ coiled

13. _____ project

14. _____ with

15. _____ small

16. _____ worse

17. _____ project

18. _____ tight

19. _____ called

20. _____ talked

Name _____ Date _____

Unit 6   *Alice the Artist*

Proofread each sentence below. Each has a Spelling
word in it. Circle the Spelling word, and then write
it correct spelling on the line.

1. I don't think it's a good idea to move away. _____

2. Do you denie the allegations? _____

3. Could you project your voice for your presentation? _____

4. She was disappoiinted with her grade on the test. _____

5. Christie came down wit the flu. _____

6. My shoes are too tite. _____

7. I would like to try skiing next winter. _____

8. Lily's mother tallked to our class about how to earn a good grade.

_____

9. The boy has falen asleep on the couch. _____

10. Collin gave the dog a batth. _____

11. He did a whorse job cleaning than I did. _____

12. Janice is thrifte and saves a lot of money. _____

13. Could you turn of the other light? _____

14. You can wip your hands on the towel. _____

15. The living room wal is covered with family pictures. _____

16. My father taaught me how to speak Italian. _____

17. The coyled roped is on the ground. _____

18. There's a smal scratch in the table. _____

19. Our history project is due on Friday. _____

20. My mother should have called us to dinner by now. _____

A storm was about to move into the city. Tucker and   1–11
his family were at home. Dad was planting roses in the   12–22
garden. Mom was on the porch fixing a broken spoke   23–32
on the wheel of Tucker's bike. Tucker was doing chores   33–42
around the house.   43–45

"Tucker," said Mom. "This will be a bad, fast storm,   46–55
but it might have a nice surprise at the end."   56–65

The storm came fast. White clouds blew past,   66–73
followed by dark, gray clouds. "Those clouds are ready   74–82
to explode with rain," said Dad. At that exact moment,   83–92
the rain started to fall. Thunder filled Tucker's ears. His   93–102
cat, Wheaty, was so scared she ran to Tucker. "Don't be   103–113
afraid, Wheaty," Tucker whispered to his furry feline   114–121
friend. "Mom says the storm has a nice surprise at the   122–132
end."   133–133

It thundered and rained for an hour or so. Tucker had   134–144
just started to doze off when he noticed that the sun was   145–156
coming out. "Tucker!" Mom yelled. "Come to the porch   157–165
and see the surprise."   166–169

In the sky was a bright rainbow! "See, Wheaty, the   170–179
storm was worth it," said Tucker.   180–185

I read this
○ silently.   ○ aloud.   ○ with a partner.   ○ with the teacher.

Unit 6 • *Alice the Artist* • STORY 4

Phyllis went to the library to quickly look for some	1–10
books about photography. She had gotten a camera for	11–19
her birthday and wanted to learn how to take effective	20–29
photos. The problem was that there were over a hundred	30–39
books about photography. Phyllis asked for help. The	40–47
librarian understood what Phyllis wanted and found a	48–55
few good books for her.	56–60
Several hours later, Phyllis had looked over most of	61–69
the books. She left the library and took her camera back	70–80
to her neighborhood. Phyllis took snapshots all around	81–88
her neighborhood. She took a snapshot of the crooked	89–97
wood on an old telephone pole. She took a photo of an	98–109
antenna on the hood of a car. She took photos of all sorts	110–122
of other things she had observed before and thought	123–131
might look neat.	132–134
Her older sister arrived with her adorable new baby	135–143
boy. Phyllis took a photo of her nephew. That was going	144–154
to be a good photo. Phyllis thinks she might like to earn a	155–167
living by being a photographer.	168–172

I read this
○ silently.   ○ aloud.   ○ with a partner.   ○ with the teacher.

Unit 6 • *A Great Idea*

1. _____ humor
2. _____ undone
3. _____ more
4. _____ visual
5. _____ employed
6. _____ unlike
7. _____ questions
8. _____ subject
9. _____ incredible
10. _____ drums
11. _____ speak
12. _____ morning
13. _____ tricks
14. _____ interpret
15. _____ draw
16. _____ utilities
17. _____ transferred
18. _____ kitten
19. _____ destroyed
20. _____ duck

Unit 6 • *A Great Idea*

Proofread each sentence below. Each has a Spelling word in it. Circle the Spelling word, and then write its correct spelling on the line.

1. Some questions on the test were very difficult. _____

2. Troy's druums will move into the basement. _____

3. The cost of uetilities has increased. _____

4. Our hotel room has an inncredible view. _____

5. The ducck is swimming on the pond. _____

6. We should see each other mor often. _____

7. I can't interrpret his writing. _____

8. He didn't see the huemor in the situation. _____

9. Those people are completely unnlike each other. _____

10. The fire destroiyed the garage. _____

11. David added visual images to his report. _____

12. Her hair had come undun. _____

13. Morgan held the citten. _____

14. Many people who will earn promotions are employed by the company.

_____

15. Her actions speek louder than her words. _____

16. Cody trannsferred to a different school. _____

17. She uses a ruler to draww lines. _____

18. What is the subbject of your report? _____

19. Are you playing triks on us? _____

20. We had only pancakes this morning for breakfast. _____

While the stars were shining in the sky, Bob and Betty	1–11
Blanco went for a midnight ride in their boat. The boat	12–22
was named *The Easy Life*. Bob and his wife Betty bought	23–33
it when they retired.	34–37
As the boat bobbed in the lake, Bob and Betty lay	38–48
back to silently gaze at the sky. They felt like the only	49–60
people in the world. After a while, Betty asked Bob	61–70
whether he could find patterns in the stars. Betty said	71–80
that if you made imaginary lines between certain stars,	81–89
you could make shapes.	90–93
Bob pointed at some stars on the right side of the	94–104
night sky. "Those look like a spider," said Bob.	105–113
"I see stars that look like a bike," said Betty. "I also	114–125
see what looks like a pine tree, and there is a lady with a	126–139
kite."	140–140
"If you look high over there," said Bob as he pointed	141–151
to a bright star, "you can see the Big Dipper."	152–161
Bob and Betty enjoyed their night. It was time for	162–171
them to head back. They had a dock behind their house.	172–182
To park the boat, they had to wrap a rope around a post.	183–195
Bob and Betty Blanco had worked hard all their lives.	196–205
Now they enjoyed their life of retirement together.	206–213

I read this
O silently.   O aloud.   O with a partner.   O with the teacher.

Shelly Zack ran a newspaper called *The Marsville*   1–8
Ledger. She made all the choices on what stories the   9–18
newspaper would print. Today she printed a story on   19–27
the turmoil that went on in the local dress factory. The   28–38
factory kept using bad zippers. A number of customers   39–47
had phoned in complaints. It was a hard story to tell.   48–58
Shelly hoped it did not spoil the factory's business.   59–67

Also in the newspaper was a story about the jet   68–77
stream that was going to send a blizzard into Marsville.   78–87
The story listed good ways for citizens to avoid blizzard   88–97
dangers, and it included facts on how to measure the   98–107
snow. The tips were not really news, but Shelly thought   108–117
people should read them.   118–121

The Marsville Ledger also lets others voice their   122–129
thoughts. Shelly decided to print a letter from a woman   130–139
who was disappointed with Marsville's mayor,   140–145
Ned Roiceman, for his choice not to put funding toward   146–155
the Marsville Zoo. Shelly realized the mayor would be   156–164
unhappy about the letter.   165–168

It would surprise readers to find out that Shelly   169–177
Zack liked to relax in bed and do the paper's crossword   178–188
puzzle. It was never easy, but she liked that there were no   189–200
choices to make. Either the answer was right or wrong.   201–210
She already made enough hard choices.   211–216

I read this
◯ silently.   ◯ aloud.   ◯ with a partner.   ◯ with the teacher.

Unit 6 • *A Great Idea*

Cut out the boxes on this page to make your own
set of Sight Word cards. The following Sight Words
are reviewed in this lesson.

measure	
Unit 6, Lesson 11	Unit 6, Lesson 11
only	
Unit 6, Lesson 11	Unit 6, Lesson 11
people	
Unit 6, Lesson 11	Unit 6, Lesson 11
Unit 6, Lesson 11	Unit 6, Lesson 11

Unit 6 • *Wonderful Stevie Wonder*

Cut out the boxes on this page to make your own
set of Sight Word cards. The following Sight Words
are reviewed in this lesson.

become Unit 6, Lesson 16	Unit 6, Lesson 16
off Unit 6, Lesson 16	Unit 6, Lesson 16
Unit 6, Lesson 16	Unit 6, Lesson 16
Unit 6, Lesson 16	Unit 6, Lesson 16

Name _____ Date _____

Unit 6 • *Wonderful Stevie Wonder*

1. _____ wrestling

2. _____ lengthen

3. _____ reign

4. _____ alone

5. _____ wrap

6. _____ bake

7. _____ famous

8. _____ acorn

9. _____ rain

10. _____ photo

11. _____

_____ whales

12. _____ save

13. _____ look

14. _____ where

15. _____ table

16. _____

_____ soften

17. _____ hood

18. _____ wrote

19. _____ hazardous

20. _____ father

Unit 6 • *Wonderful Stevie Wonder*

Proofread each sentence below. Each has a Spelling word in it. Circle the Spelling word, and then write its correct spelling on the line.

1. I sav money in my piggy bank. _____

2. She doesn't lok well. _____

3. Were do you live? _____

4. Dinner is on the tayble. _____

5. Conner is on the wrestling team with people from his community.

_____

6. Dad is going to lengthin his trip to Detroit. _____

7. The royal family will reign in England. _____

8. We saw beluga wales at the aquarium. _____

9. They tried to softin the blow of the bad news. _____

10. My gray sweater has a hod. _____

11. Those chemicals can be hazardous to your health. _____

12. I helped my faather clean the basement. _____

13. My sister asked me to leave her allone. _____

14. Before we go out, I will wrrap the baby in a blanket. _____

15. Heather and I are going to bak a cake after we measure the ingredients.

_____

16. I put the foto in the frame. _____

17. Our soccer game will become delayed because of the rain. _____

18. The man is a famous author. _____

19. The boy picked up an aycorn off of the ground. _____

20. Jason rote a short story for his only English class. _____

Stewart had to write a report for class about the use	1–11
of fuel in the United States. It was due the next afternoon	12–23
in science class. He decided to list some of the different	24–34
ways fuel is used.	35–38
He started at the airport. Airlines use fuel for their	39–48
planes. Long flights take more fuel, and short flights	49–57
use less fuel. Stewart explained that the workers at the	58–67
airport wear uniforms and use huge hoses to pump fuel	68–77
into the planes.	78–80
Electricity is also a fuel. Computers, lamps, TVs, and	81–89
many other things use electricity to run. That's why there	90–99
are so many cords all around!	100–105
There are all sorts of uses for different forms of fuel.	106–116
Even a power leaf blower uses fuel. It's a form of the fuel	117–129
used by the airplanes.	130–133
"Humans use fuel, too" wrote Stewart. The things	134–141
we eat and drink become the body's fuel. If a person	142–152
participates in sports, he or she needs more fuel.	153–161
Stewart reread what he wrote. "I hope," he said to	162–171
himself, "this report has enough content to fuel a good	172–181
grade!"	182–182

I read this
○ silently.   ○ aloud.   ○ with a partner.   ○ with the teacher.

Unit 6 • *Wonderful Stevie Wonder* • STORY 8

Down by the lake is a trail that runs around the forest	1–12
and back to Bob and Betty Blanco's house. Bob and Betty	13–23
like to be outside, and the trail allows them to frequently	24–34
enjoy a quick, quiet hike.	35–39
Their four-year-old granddaughter, Tina, likes to walk	40–46
with them. When Tina heard ducks quacking on the lake,	47–56
she said, "Grandmother, I know what the quacks mean!"	57–65
"What?" asked Betty.	66–68
"I'm not allowed to tell," said Tina in a serious tone.	69–79
Betty and Bob smiled at their cute granddaughter.	80–87
On the trail are different kinds of blossoms. Tina likes	88–97
to look at and smell the wild roses. She blows the seeds	98–109
from dandelions. She also invents names for the flowers.	110–118
On a hike last week, she said, "That is a quilt posie. That	119–131
brown flower over there is called a mouse flower. This	132–141
flower is big and orange, so it's called a tomato flower."	142–152
On the same hike, Tina saw an owl in the forest. It	153–164
was little ways off the trail. When it said "Whoo! Whoo!"	165–175
Tina said it sounded loud. Then she yelled back, "Me!	176–185
Me!"	186–186
Betty and Bob chuckled. Bob said, "Tina, you are the	187–196
queen of the trail!"	197–200

I read this
○ silently.　　○ aloud.　　○ with a partner.　　○ with the teacher.

Unit 6 • *Into the Sky*

1. _____ top

2. _____ bilingual

3. _____ pool

4. _____ unison

5. _____ whole

6. _____ tricycle

7. _____ over

8. _____ knew

9. _____ complaint

10. _____ charity

11. _____ crows

12. _____

    _____ multipurpose

13. _____ too

14. _____ boots

15. _____ home

16. _____ architect

17. _____ hosting

18. _____ stew

19. _____ hope

20. _____ tomorrow

Unit 6 • *Into the Sky*

Proofread each sentence below. Each has a Spelling word in it. Circle the Spelling word, and then write its correct spelling on the line.

1. Grandma is coming to visit tomorro. _____

2. There's a fundraiser for the charitty tonight. _____

3. Would you like to come ovver to my house? _____

4. This multipurpose tool is very handy. _____

5. A person who is beilingual speaks two languages. _____

6. I took my dirty bots off and put them outside. _____

7. My mother is hoosting a dinner party on Saturday. _____

8. The water in the pol is warm. _____

9. Ava's triicycle is on the patio. _____

10. I hop it doesn't rain today. _____

11. I need hole milk for the recipe. _____

12. I wish I kneew where I left my keys. _____

13. Syndney is at the top of her class. _____

14. "Hello," Al and Jess said in unnison. _____

15. We had steew for dinner. _____

16. The woman called the company to report a commplaint. _____

17. The black croows have a nest in the tree. _____

18. I heard Carrie is going to take ballet lessons to. _____

19. Do you think Evan is at hom? _____

20. Someday, Anna would like to become an architect. _____

Name _____ Date _____

Long ago, there was an open field between the green | 1–10
houses on Dean Street. Dan lived in the green house to | 11–21
the east of the field, and Hector lived in the green house | 22–33
to the west. Because Dan and Hector were born thirteen | 34–43
days apart, they were always in the same grade and | 44–53
became great buddies. | 54–56

When they were both three years old, their parents | 57–65
helped the boys plant a cherry tree in the open field. | 66–76

Dan and Hector enjoyed the tree. As it grew bigger, | 77–86
they picked cherries and learned to make cherry jelly. It | 87–96
was their favorite spread for toasted bread. | 97–103

They liked to sit under the tree on hot days. The tree's | 104–115
branches would shield the boys from the heat of the | 116–125
midday sun. While sitting there, Dan and Hector planned | 126–134
ahead for their adult lives. They had a secret plan for | 135–145
joining in a successful business. | 146–150

When they grew up, they acted on their plans and | 151–160
started selling Royal Cherry Jelly made with a secret | 161–169
formula they invented. Soon they owned big jelly | 170–177
factories and fields of cherry trees. They shared their | 178–186
success with their families and the community. | 187–193

If you visit Dean Street now, you will see a monument | 194–204
to Dan, Hector, and the cherry tree. | 205–211

I read this
O silently.   O aloud.   O with a partner.   O with the teacher.

There was a woman named Colleen Moose who used	1–9
to live in a houseboat docked on the river. Colleen's boat	10–20
was named *Smooth Stew*. Colleen liked to keep her boat	21–30
clean, so she would choose a few of the kids living in	31–42
Rockville to clean *Smooth Stew*. All of the kids heard	43–52
about *Smooth Stew* and liked to work for Colleen.	53–61
Colleen would get all kinds of cleaning supplies. She	62–70
had special soap for the roof of the boat and special	71–81
shampoo for the deck too. At about noon, Colleen would	82–91
head into Rockville and leave the kids to collaborate on	92–101
cleaning the boat.	102–104
The bigger kids thought it was pretty cool that	105–113
Colleen Moose would leave them alone to clean. They	114–122
knew that Colleen trusted them.	123–127
After a few hours, Colleen Moose would return to find	128–137
her boat clean as new. The kids would even tighten loose	138–148
screws. Colleen would reach into her pocket and pay all	149–158
the kids. On the way back into Rockville, Colleen would	159–168
take the kids to the swimming pool as a reward.	169–178
When the kids grew up and left Rockville, they always	179–188
remembered how much they liked Colleen Moose.	189–195

I read this
O silently.   O aloud.   O with a partner.   O with the teacher.

Name _____ Date _____

Unit 6 • *Into the Sky*

Cut out the boxes on this page to make your own
set of Sight Word cards. The following Sight Words
are reviewed in this lesson.

heard

Unit 6, Lesson 21

Unit 6, Lesson 21

woman

Unit 6, Lesson 21

Unit 6, Lesson 21

Unit 6, Lesson 21

Unit 6, Lesson 21

Unit 6, Lesson 21

Unit 6, Lesson 21

Unit 6 • *Detroit Industry*

Cut out the boxes on this page to make your own
set of Sight Word cards. The following Sight Words
are reviewed in this lesson.

father	
Unit 6, Lesson 26	Unit 6, Lesson 26
mother	
Unit 6, Lesson 26	Unit 6, Lesson 26
Unit 6, Lesson 26	Unit 6, Lesson 26
Unit 6, Lesson 26	Unit 6, Lesson 26

DECODABLE STORIES AND SPELLING

Name _____ Date _____

Unit 6 • *Detroit Industry*

1. _____ part
2. _____ rewrite
3. _____ colorful
4. _____ next
5. _____ avoid
6. _____ farther
7. _____ bark
8. _____ leather
9. _____ read
10. _____ yet
11. _____ grapes
12. _____ soiled
13. _____ weather
14. _____ actor
15. _____
_____ retake
16. _____ royal
17. _____ nice
18. _____ helpful
19. _____ green
20. _____ know

Name _____ Date _____

Unit 6 • *Detroit Industry*

Proofread each sentence below. Each has a Spelling word in it. Circle the Spelling word, and then write its correct spelling on the line.

1. I am going to avoid Hal because he is not nice to me. _____

2. Dogs often barrk at mail carriers. _____

3. Have you read the book for English class yeet? _____

4. The wheather man said that it would be sunny today. _____

5. I don't now how to change a tire. _____

6. My father forgot to buy garapes at the store. _____

7. My new dress is royyal blue. _____

8. I'm going to reewrite my speech. _____

9. Lou had to reetake his driver's test. _____

10. The artist's painting is very colerful. _____

11. In the spring, the grass turns green. _____

12. Emily has red lether shoes. _____

13. The librarian was very helpfull. _____

14. The mechanic needs to order the parrt for our car. _____

15. Neext time we visit Florida, we're going to the aquarium. _____

16. I walked further today than I did yesterday. _____

17. Newspapers can be read online. _____

18. The mud soiiled my new pants. _____

19. What is the name of the acter in this movie? _____

20. My mother said to be nice to your brother. _____

Phil thought it would be a good day to take a walk   1–12
down to the general store on Gopher Avenue. Phil was   13–22
having thirteen buddies over for dinner. He wanted to   23–31
make an enjoyable dinner.   32–35

He thought that a pheasant dinner would be nice. A   36–45
pheasant is a bird similar to a turkey. Phil recalled seeing 46–56
pheasant for sale at the store. He also wanted to grab a   57–68
small can of spice, some raw oysters, a celery stalk, soy   69–79
sauce, and some walnuts.   80–83

"Boy," thought Phil, "I can't wait until all my pals taste 84–94
this dinner."   95–96

Phil bought all the things he needed and zipped back   97–106
to his house on Decoy Street. He talked to his mother and   107–118
father on the phone while he hurried to make all the food. 119–130
Phil sometimes sought advice from his parents about   131–138
cooking.   139–139

All of Phil's pals arrived for dinner. They got stalled in 140–150
the hallway of Phil's house when a pal took some photos.   151–161
Then they all enjoyed talking for a short time. When   162–171
they finally sat to eat, they enjoyed Phil's dinner. They   172–181
all thought it was a great meal. Phil's dinner party was a 182–193
triumph.   194–194

I read this
○ silently.   ○ aloud.   ○ with a partner.   ○ with the teacher.

There was a big sale going on at Cecil's Pet Shop.   1–11
Zeke wanted to go to the sale to see whether he could   12–23
find some new fish for his fish tank. So Zeke hopped on   24–35
his nice bike and rode onto the cement of the sidewalk.   36–46

After a little bit of a ride, Zeke was in the center of   47–59
town. He found Cecil's Pet Shop and locked his bike to   60–70
the fence in front of Cecil's.   71–76

Zeke looked around. He saw a pink pig that a person   77–87
could take home as a pet. There was a cage of mice. Of   88–100
course, Cecil had lots of cats and dogs in his pet shop   101–112
too. Then Zeke saw the yellow fish beside the cage that   113–123
held a singing bird.   124–127

"I'd like to take that yellow fish there," Zeke told   128–137
Cecil. Cecil took the fish from the tank and placed it in a 138–150
plastic bin made for carrying fish. Zeke looked in the bin   151–161
at the face of the fish. "I'll name him Binny," said Zeke.   162–173

Zeke fastened the bin to his bike and walked the bike   174–184
home slowly so that Binny the fish would stay in the   185–195
plastic bin.   196–197

I read this
○ silently.   ○ aloud.   ○ with a partner.   ○ with the teacher.

Spelling Rules

General Spelling Rules for Most Words

- All words have at least one vowel.
- Most words have at least one consonant.
- Every syllable has a vowel or the letter *y*.
- Many words are spelled exactly as they sound.
- Some words are exceptions to spelling rules and must be memorized.

Consonant Spellings

Most consonants sound like their letter names.

- /b/ is spelled *b* as in *bad*
- /d/ is spelled *d* as in *dash*
- /f/ is spelled *f* as in *fast*
- /j/ is spelled *j* as in *jog*
- /k/ is spelled *k* as in *kiss*
- /l/ is spelled *l* as in *lot*
- /m/ is spelled *m* as in *map*

- /n/ is spelled *n* as in *nest*
- /p/ is spelled *p* as in *pin*
- /r/ is spelled *r* as in *rug*
- /s/ is spelled *s* as in *sand*
- /t/ is spelled *t* as in *tip*
- /v/ is spelled *v* as in *vat*
- /z/ is spelled *z* as in *zip*

Some consonants do not sound like their letter names.

- /h/ does not sound like the letter *h*. *(hill)*
- /w/ does not sound like the letter *w*. *(wish)*
- /y/ does not sound like the letter *y*. *(yell)*
- There are hard and soft sounds for the letter *c*.
    hard *c*: /k/ is spelled *c* as in *can*
    soft *c*: /s/ is spelled *c* as in *cell*
- There are hard and soft sounds for the letter *g*.
    hard *g*: /g/ is spelled *g* as in *gum*
    soft *g*: /j/ is spelled *g* as in *gym*

Consonant Blends

Consonant blends are two- or three-letter combinations in which each letter can be heard.

- Three main groupings are the *s*-blends, *r*-blends, and *l*-blends.

- Two-letter *s*-blend /sl/ is spelled *sl* as in <u>sl</u>ip.
      /sp/ is spelled *sp* as in <u>sp</u>eak
      /sk/ is spelled *sk* as in <u>sk</u>y
      /sk/ is spelled *sc* in <u>sc</u>are
      /sm/ is spelled *sm* as in <u>sm</u>ell
      /sn/ is spelled *sn* as in <u>sn</u>ow
      /st/ is spelled *st* as in <u>st</u>ack
      /sw/ is spelled *sw* as in <u>sw</u>im

- The blends *sc* and *sk* both spell the /sk/ sound. *(scan, skip)*

- When you hear the /sk/ sound at the end of a word, spell it *sk*, not *sc*. *(risk,* not *risc)*

- Only a few words have *sp* at the end, such as *wasp* and *lisp*.

- Three-letter *s*-blend /skr/ is spelled *scr* as in <u>scr</u>eam.
      /spl/ is spelled *spl* as in <u>spl</u>it
      /spr/ is spelled *spr* as in <u>spr</u>ay
      /str/ is spelled *str* as in <u>str</u>ing

- Blends found at the ends of words:

/ft/ is spelled *ft* as in *gi<u>ft</u>*	/ld/ is spelled *ld* as in *ba<u>ld</u>*
/lf/ is spelled *lf* as in *e<u>lf</u>*	/lk/ is spelled *lk* as in *mi<u>lk</u>*
/lp/ is spelled *lp* as in *he<u>lp</u>*	/lt/ is spelled *lt* as in *wi<u>lt</u>*

- The *l* is silent in *half* and *calf*.

- The final-consonant blends *mp, nd, ng, nk,* and *nt* are found at the end of one-syllable words. Most often, the vowel that comes before the blend has a short-vowel sound.

Consonant Digraphs are the letter combinations *ch, qu, th, wh, sh, ph,* and *gh* that stand for a single sound.

- *qu, wh,* and *ph* are usually found at the beginning of a word.
- The letter *q* is almost always followed by the letter *u,* as in *quick.*
- *th* can be "voiced" as in *then* or "unvoiced" as in *thank.*
- Some words, like *shred,* combine three consonants to form a consonant blend.

Consonant Choices

- The most common spelling for the /s/ sound is *s,* as in *simmer.* Other spellings are *ss, se,* and *ce,* as in *cross, once,* and *horse.* When the /s/ sound is followed by the letters *i, e, or y,* it is often spelled *c* or *sc,* as in *city* or *science.*
- The /k/ sound can be spelled *c* or *k* at the beginning of words such as *kite* and *cake.* A few words have the /k/ sound spelled *ch,* as in *chorus.* The /k/ sound spelled *ck* is found at the end of a word, as in *back.*
- The /j/ sound is usually spelled *j* as in *joke.* At the end of some words, such as *fudge* and *huge,* /j/ can be spelled *dge* or *ge.* Before the letters *e, y,* or *i,* the /j/ sound can be spelled *g,* as in *giant, gem,* or *gym.*

Double-Consonant Spellings

- Most double-consonant patterns occur in the middle or final position of a word, as in *stall, pizza,* and *lettuce.*
- The most common double consonants in the final position are *ff, ss,* and *ll,* as in *cliff, cross,* and *still.*
- Double consonants are rarely found at the beginning of a word, as in *llama* and *Lloyd.*

Silent Letters

- *g* is silent in the blend *gn* at the beginning or end of a word, such as *gnome* or *sign.*
- *k* is silent in the blend *kn* at the beginning of a word, such as *knight.*
- *b* is silent in the blend *mb* at the end of a word, such as *thumb.*
- *w* is silent in the blend *wr* at the beginning of a word, such as *write.*
- The *g* is not silent in a word in which *gn* is divided into syllables, as in *signal.*
- Some words have mb followed by le, in which the b is not silent, as in *thimble, tumble,* and *crumble.*

SHORT-VOWEL SOUND/SPELLINGS

Short-vowel sound/spellings are more predictable than long-vowel sound/spellings.

- Short-vowel sounds are most often found in words beginning with a vowel, such as *up, at,* and *end,* or words with *vowel-consonant* endings, such as *cup, bat,* and *lend.*
- Some short-vowel sounds are spelled with two or more letters, such as *bread* and *laugh.*
- Short vowels have many simple spelling patterns, such as *at, in, ot, et,* and *ug.*

The /a/ Sound

- /a/ is spelled *a,* as in *cat.*
- /a/ can also be spelled *au,* as in *laugh,* or *ai,* as in *plaid.*

The /e/ Sound

- /e/ is most often spelled *e,* as in *bed.*
- /e/ can be spelled *ea* in the middle of a word, as in *bread* or *head.*

The /i/ Sound

- /i/ is most often spelled *i,* as in *did.*
- When *y* is found in the middle of a word, it acts like a vowel. It usually makes the /i/ sound, as in *system.*
- /i/ is sometimes spelled *i-consonant-e,* as in the words *give* and *live.*

The /o/ Sound

- /o/ is usually spelled *o,* as in *got.*
- /o/ can be spelled *o, aw, oa, au,* and *ou,* as in *dog, awful, broad, caught,* and *brought.*

The /u/ Sound

- /u/ is usually spelled *u,* as in *fun.*
- /u/ can be spelled *o,* as in *son,* or *o-consonant-e,* as in *glove* and *love.*

The /oi/ Sound

- /oi/ is spelled *oy* or *oi,* as in *boy, oyster, boil,* and *oil.*
- The *oi* spelling is found at the beginning and in the middle of words.
- The *oy* spelling is mostly found at the end of a word and sometimes at the end of a syllable, as in *loyal.*

The /o͞o/ Sound

- /o͞o/ can be spelled *u* or *oo,* as in *put* and *book.*
- In a few words, /o͞o/ can be spelled *ou,* as in *could.*

LONG-VOWEL SOUND/SPELLINGS

Long vowels sound like the letter names. When long-vowel sounds are spelled with two vowels, usually the first vowel is heard and the second vowel is silent.

Vowel-consonant-e

- Many long-vowel sounds have the common *vowel-consonant-e* spelling pattern in which the *e* is silent, as in the word *date*.

The /ā/ Sound

- /ā/ is spelled *a*, *a-consonant-e*, *ai*, and *ay*, as in *agent, base, raid*, and *today*. The *ay* spelling is found at the end of words or syllables, and the *ai* spelling is found in the middle of words.

The /ē/ Sound

- /ē/ is often spelled *e*, *e-consonant-e*, *ee*, *ea*, and *y* at the end of words, such as *be, here, agree, easy*, and *happy*.
- /ē/ is spelled *ei* in a few words, such as *receive*, but also *ie*, as in *pierce*. Remember the rhyme: "Write *i* before *e*, except after *c*, or when it sounds like /ā/ as in *neighbor* and *weigh*."
- /ē/ can be spelled *i-consonant-e* in words such as *machine* and *police*.

The /ī/ Sound

- /ī/ is spelled *i*, *i-consonant-e*, *igh*, *i-consonant-consonant*, and *y*, as in *icy, site, high, find*, and *dry*.

The /ō/ Sound

- /ō/ is spelled *o*, *o-consonant-e*, *oa*, *o-consonant-consonant*, and *ow*, as in *pony, bone, boat, revolt*, and *snow*.

The /ū/ Sound

- /ū/ is spelled *u*, *ue*, or *u-consonant-e*, as in *unit, cue*, and *cube*.

The /o͞o/ Sound

- /o͞o/ can be spelled *oo* in the middle of a word such as *tool*, *u* in the *u-consonant-e* pattern as in *tune*, or *ew* at the end of a word such as *new*.
- /o͞o/ can also be spelled *ough* as in *through*.

THE SCHWA SOUND

Unaccented syllables have a vowel sound called a schwa that is represented by a vowel. A variety of vowels can stand for the schwa sound. Visualizing how a word should look or over-pronouncing the ending as you spell it may help.

Schwa *-ant, -ent, -ance, -ence*

- The endings *-ant* and *-ent* add the meaning "one who" to a word.
- The endings *-ance* and *-ence* add the meaning "state or quality of" to a word.
- More words end in *-ent* and *-ence* than in *-ant* and *-ance*.
- Visualizing how the word should look can help you learn to spell words with these endings.

The /sh/ sound spelled *ti, ci, si*

- Drop the silent *e* before adding the ending. *race, racial*
- Words that end in *c* or *ce* have the *ci* pattern. *finance, financial*
- Words that end in *s* usually contain the *si* pattern. *impress, impression*
- Words that end in *t* often have the *ti* pattern. *reject, rejection*
- Some words have consonant spelling changes before the endings are added, such as *emit* and *emission*.

Schwa *-el, -al, -le, -il, -le*

- Most of the time, the /əl/ sound at the end of a word is spelled *-le. little, circle*
- Verbs and action words that end with the /əl/ sound have the *-le* spelling. *dazzle*
- Words that have the *-al* spelling for the /əl/ sound are usually nouns or adjectives, words that describe nouns. *animal, petal, final, signal*
- Usually, words that end with the /əl/ sound spelled *-ile* are adjectives. *agile, fertile*
- Words with final syllables that have the /əl/ sound can also be spelled *-el* or *-il*. Usually these words are nouns. *towel, label, gerbil, pencil*
- In a few words, the /əl/ final syllable is spelled *-ol. capitol*

STRUCTURAL SPELLING PATTERNS

Plurals

- Add -*s* to most nouns to make them plural. *(cat + s = cats)*
- Add -*es* to words that end in *ch, sh, s, ss, x, z,* or *zz*.
- Noticing the syllables in the singular and plural forms of a word can help you know whether to add -*s* or -*es*. When -*es* is added, it usually adds another syllable.

Irregular Plurals

- For some words that end in *f* or *fe*, change the *f* to a *v* and add -*es*.
- Some plurals are spelled the same as the singular form, such as *deer*.
- The spelling changes in the plural form of some words, such as *tooth* and *teeth*.
- For a word that ends in *consonant-o*, add -*es*. If a word ends in *vowel-o*, -*s* is usually added.

Adding -*ed* and -*ing*

- The ending -*ed* is added to most words to show an action that happened in the past.
- The ending -*ing* is added to a word to show an action that is happening in the present.
- Drop the silent *e* before adding -*ed* and -*ing* to words.

Adding -*er* and -*est*

- The endings -*er* and -*est* are added to words to show comparisons, such as *whiter* and *whitest*.
- Drop the silent *e* before adding these endings to words.

Double Final Consonants

- Use the "1-1-1 Check" to double a final consonant:
  1. Does the word have 1 syllable? *fun*
  2. Does the word have 1 vowel? *fun*
  3. Does the word end with 1 consonant? *fun*
  Double the final consonant if all the answers are yes. *funny*
- Double the final consonant if the last syllable of the word is accented or stressed.
- Do not double the final consonant if the last syllable is unstressed.
- Do not double the final consonant for words ending in a short vowel and *x*.

MEANING PATTERNS

Word Families *-ous*

- Words that end in *-ous* are common.
- If a word ends in *e*, drop the *e* before adding *-ous*.
- Change *y* to *i* before adding *-ous* to a word that ends in *y*.
- *-ous* added to a word creates an adjective.
- There are a few words with the soft *g* sound, as in *courageous*, in which the final *e* is not dropped.

Vowel-Sound Changes

- When the vowel sound in a base word changes because of an added ending, think of the base-word spelling, and use the same vowel that is in the base word. *(major, majority)*

Contractions

- A contraction is a word formed from two or more words. When the words are joined together, some letters are taken out, and an apostrophe (') marks the place.
- Only one letter is taken out of some contractions.

$$I\ am - a = I'm$$

- Many letters are taken out of some contractions.

$$I\ would - woul = I'd$$

- The first word in the pair that makes a contraction usually keeps all of its letters.
- Entire words are left out of some contractions.
  (of the clock – f and the = o'clock)
- Some contractions are homophones. *(I'll, aisle; he'd, heed)*
- Make sure you put the apostrophe (') in the right place.
- Leaving out the apostrophe can result in a different word. The word *I'll* becomes the word *ill*.
- Only one contraction, *I'm*, is made with the word *am*.
- Only one contraction, *let's*, is made with the word *us*.
- Some contractions look the same but mean two different things. *He'd* can mean, "he would" or "he had."
- The contraction for *will not* changes the spelling and the sound of the omitted letters to become *won't*.

DECODABLE STORIES AND SPELLING

Compound Words

- Compound words are made up of two smaller, complete words. None of the letters are taken out of the words. The spelling of each word stays the same. For example, *news* and *paper* combine to form the compound word *newspaper*.

German and French Spelling Patterns

- Many German words can be recognized by the /ur/ sound spelled -*er* or -*ur*.

    hamb<u>ur</u>ger   frankf<u>ur</u>ter

- Some German words end with the /əl/ sound spelled -*el* or have the /ow/ sound spelled *au* or *ow*.

    s<u>au</u>erkraut   pretz<u>el</u>   ch<u>ow</u>der

- Many French words can be recognized by the /ā/ sound spelled *é, ée, et,* and *ai*. The *t* is silent in *et*.

    entr<u>ée</u>   gourm<u>et</u>   mayonn<u>ai</u>se   caf<u>é</u>

- German words often stress the root syllable.
    French words often stress the final syllable.
    German: hamster (ham'•ster)
    French: ballet (bal•let')

Italian and Spanish Spelling Patterns

- Many Italian and Spanish words end with a vowel.
    Italian: *lasagn<u>a</u>*   Spanish: *avocad<u>o</u>*
- Some Italian and Spanish words contain double consonants.
    Italian: *pi<u>zz</u>a*   Spanish: *bu<u>rr</u>o*
- The double consonant *ll* in some Spanish words makes the /y/ sound, not the /l/ sound.

    torti<u>ll</u>a

Latin Spelling Patterns

- Latin roots are meaningful word parts that combine with words.

Root	Meaning
scribe, script	to write
form	a shape
sent, sens	to feel
rupt	to break
equa, equi	even
min	to make smaller
mit	to send
bene, beni	well
aud	to hear
port	to carry
dic, dict	to speak
gram	to write

- Some Latin patterns sound like others, which can make them tricky to spell.

Greek Spelling Patterns

- Understanding Greek word patterns and their meanings can help you spell many new words.

Root	Meaning
geo	earth
tele	far off
phon, phone	sounds
hydro	water
micro	small
aster, astr	star
centr	center
phobia	fear
graph	to write
bi, bio	life
cycl	circle
phys	nature
photo	light

- Many Greek roots spell the /f/ sound with the letters *ph*. When you hear the /f/ sound in an unfamiliar word with a Greek root, spell it with a *ph*.

Oral Fluency Chart

Date	Total Words Read	Number of Errors	Accuracy Rate

Name _____ Date _____

Trace or photocopy the grid on this page. Then fill in
each box with a Spelling word. Cut out the boxes to make
your own set of Spelling word cards.